Country Boy

Country Boy

Adventures from an Untroubled Childhood

Dan Prusi

Copyright © 2002 by Daniel W. Prusi.

Library of Congress Number: 2002092247
ISBN :   Hardcover   1-4010-5982-1
           Softcover   1-4010-5981-3

All rights reserved. No part of this book may be reproduced or transmitted in any form or by any means, electronic or mechanical, including photocopying, recording, or by any information storage and retrieval system, without permission in writing from the copyright owner.

This book was printed in the United States of America.

To order additional copies of this book, contact:
Xlibris Corporation
1-888-795-4274
www.Xlibris.com
Orders@Xlibris.com
15419

Contents

Acknowledgments 9
Foreword 11
1 : Bellevue Location 14
2 : Life in the Valley 20
3 : Young Legs 30
4 : Mentoring 40
5 : Prusi and Prusi—WORMS 46
6 : Boy's Best Friend 51
7 : The Best Pond Ever 57

FAMILY PHOTO ALBUM

8 : Snow Day 78
9 : Ragamuffin Sniper 82
10 : Yodskof Space Capsule 89
11 : Young Love, First Love 94
12 : Ghosts, Goblins, and the Paranormal 98
13 : The Camp 103
14 : Christmas 108
15 : Forting Up 114
16 : The Mines 119
17 : Goodbye to Bellevue 130
18 : All Grown Up 138

FOR MOM

Acknowledgments

This story was made possible by my parents, Uncle Bill and Aunt Jennie, my seven sisters and the six cousins who grew up next door. All of them are a part of my childhood, and thus they *are* the story. Many of these folks have encouraged my writing for years, and I hope that this work will not let them down! My wife Sherilee and my children, Ben, Danny and Tara, have made my life *after* childhood as trouble free as it could be, and when there was a troubling time they shared the burden and lightened my own. My time with them is as treasured as the early days that are described in this book.

My sisters, Cheryl Prusi and Sue Johnson, and my cousins Audrey Wright and Julie Gahman, along with Julie's husband Terry, took on the task of proofreading and critiquing the manuscript. Their input was invaluable. It was Julie who first convinced me that these stories and my telling of them are worthy of appearing in print for the general public. Her encouragement made this book happen.

My sincere thanks to all of you.

Foreword

As a youngster, I made a pest of myself to my folks asking them to tell me about when they were kids. Their memories of childhood were fascinating to me because it almost seemed like they had lived like the pioneers. They shared a lot of their memories with me and seemed not a little surprised that I had any interest in what they saw as pretty uneventful stuff. For a long time I sort of viewed my own childhood as unremarkable. It was fun and for the most part carefree but I sort of thought that perhaps the years had a way of making good times look better than they actually were. There are literally millions of kids that had a childhood similar to mine. So was my childhood unremarkable? I have come to realize just how remarkable *every* happy childhood is.

I am a part of the last generation before Nintendo and Play Station came along. When I was a kid my big sisters could remember when we didn't have a television in the house and what a big event it was when the folks across the road were the first in the neighborhood to have one. We were able to get signals from one television station out of Marquette, Michigan, and on rare occasions could pick up a Green Bay, Wisconsin station. Watching that was like watching through a snowstorm, but given this was the Upper Peninsula of Michigan we saw a lot of our life that way! So we made our fun, most of it outdoors. Still we were miles ahead of where our folks had been as kids as far as toys and such, for as my Aunt Irene told me not long ago, when she and my Dad were kids they played with rocks, sticks, and "our imaginations".

I moved away from my first boyhood home when I was thirteen years old, and to be honest I was happy to do so for we were moving "to town". I was anxious to get into town then for I was beginning to take an interest in things there, thirteen year old girls not being the least significant of these. So I was happy to go. But within a year, or perhaps eighteen months, I found myself longing to be back in the country. I guess I had learned something about myself. My free hours were spent in the woods near town, and when I could, I fled to the country, usually our "camp" about twenty five miles away. Since those days I have lived in towns but very little, and whenever I did I was working on getting back to a rural lifestyle. I have been fortunate in that during almost my entire adult life I have been able to live "in the country". That little place where I grew up was pretty nice. I knew that inside, but didn't really spend time thinking about it till I was in my late teens or early twenties when my sister Cheryl and I were talking about where we grew up, and she just spoke the words describing what I held inside of me. Bellevue location was a wonderful place to grow up.

A lot of years have gone by since I fully began to appreciate that sentiment. My sisters and cousins and I have spent a lot of hours reminiscing about our childhood there. Now, in the Internet age, we recently set up a family web site where we began to write down a lot of our memories, and as we have done so we have jogged each other's memories and sort of unleashed a flood of nostalgia. It has been wonderful. While I have always enjoyed writing about this and that, I have usually just written for myself. Posting these memories on the family web site brought encouragement from my family to write even more, so here I am writing it down and having a ball doing it.

Country Boy

At the risk of sounding like the stereotypical "old timer", I grew up in simpler times. Kids then and now do foolish and dangerous things. I shudder to think of my own kids doing some of the things we tried. A lot of the things we said and did as kids seem rather shocking in today's context. In the early sixties these stunts were, for the most part, just considered "kid mischief". Today they might get a kid expelled from school or worse and get their parents in trouble with the law or with the civil courts. That is sort of a shame because most of the kids who do such things today are just doing kid mischief. In today's context they are treated like the genuinely bad people who do exist. We were politically incorrect in how we spoke, but that was just ignorance and/or innocence. I don't say that to make an excuse, but to point out that we had no malice inside of us. I think this is a case where things today are at least a little better. For example, we used the "N" word and other crude speech a lot. Again, not because of malice or to be mean, but out of ignorance, and I'm happy to have never heard my children use that term.

During the time I was growing up, nearly all my friends and classmates came from households that included a dad that worked (in an iron ore mine, for the most part) and a mom that stayed home. A very large number of my peers had (like I did) grandparents that were born in Europe and came to America with the great wave of immigrants in the first years of the last century. Most of the dads smoked, and lots of the moms didn't drive. The community and surrounding communities were built around the mining industry, and there were no big cities nearby. When the miners were on strike or laid off, which was all too often, times were difficult for a family like ours with eight children. I don't remember much about tough financial times, and I think that says a lot about my folks. They managed to make ends meet without strife within the family.

One more thing I must remind you about is that this all took place in the Upper Peninsula of Michigan. It is a world of its own. Not a bad one either.

1

Bellevue Location

About half way between the small towns of Negaunee and Palmer, Michigan there was once a large farm known as Bellevue Farm. I don't know when the farm came into being, or when it ceased to exist, but as a kid I would sometimes read about it in the "Days Gone By" section of the newspaper where they published old articles from ten, twenty, or fifty years before. I suppose I began reading the paper in about 1960, but I don't recall how old these articles were. Michigan Highway 35 connected Palmer and Negaunee, and as you drove from the former to the latter, on the right was a lovely little valley. To the left, the ground rose up gradually, and there was a railroad track and farm fields. Behind these were high hills covered with hardwood forest. The valley had a small "crick" flowing through it. It was here that Bellevue Farm had stood. When the farming operation ended, some of the buildings were torn down, and the lumber used to build one or more single-family homes. If you turned off M35 and on to the little road running down into the valley, the first home you came to was a small farmhouse with some log outbuildings. The road was lined with tall elm trees. As you reached the valley floor you crossed a couple of large concrete culverts where the crick ran under the road, and as you started to climb again you found yourself in a mini-neighborhood with three homes on the left and two on the right. All were nestled close to each other, and there were even a couple of streetlights along the road. A makeshift backboard and basketball hoop was attached to one of those big elm trees near one of the streetlights. At the edge of this little group of houses the ground rose up steeply again to rocky bluffs covered with trees. The homes themselves had fields around their yards that were slowly becoming grown in with brush or trees. I suppose these had to be the fields that were once cultivated or used as pastureland for Bellevue Farm. It was the first house on the right in this little group that I called home. Mom told me it had been built from the Bellevue Farm barn. The second house on the right belonged to my Aunt and Uncle and was filled with six cousins.

Perhaps a half-mile back towards Palmer from where you made the turn down into the valley was another similar neighborhood that was also part of Bellevue. Three homes on the right side of M35 and two on the left, one of these a dairy farm. Except for that little farmhouse in the valley, which was home to an elderly woman, and one of the houses in the other location, each home was occupied by families with at least three children. The ages were spread over a rather wide range, but most every kid in the neighborhood had several other kids close enough in age to be pals with. I recall eight kids in the neighborhood who were no more than two "grades" different than me in school. Some of the neighbors had children who were grown and had families of their own. They would visit in Bellevue, and several of the neighbor's grandchildren became our summertime playmates. Country kids usually don't mind hanging out with kids four or five years their senior or junior, so there were plenty of playmates for me and most of the others as well.

Our little home had three bedrooms, plus a sort of hallway between the two upstairs bedrooms. The hallway also served as a bedroom. There were eight of us, seven girls and me. There was no bathtub or shower in the house. We had a sauna outside that was connected to our garage. I am the fifth of the eight children, and twenty years separated the birth of my oldest and youngest sisters. Our Aunt and Uncle next door had six kids, three boys and three girls, and the time span between the oldest and youngest was a little less than that in our family. Uncle Bill was my Dad's brother, and Aunt Jennie was my Mom's sister, so we were "double" cousins. Dad's family had twelve kids and Mom's eleven, so we had quite a collection of cousins in addition to those next door. Neither Mom nor Aunt Jennie drove, and we never had more than one car in our family until long after we left Bellevue. Dad worked in an underground iron mine, and Uncle Bill was a mechanic and snowplow driver for the County. Both moms were full time homemakers.

The two families had moved to Bellevue when there were only three or four children in each household, but they had lived in the same "duplex" even before coming to Bellevue. That was a house just outside Negaunee, and one family lived in the upstairs apartment and the other downstairs. The families started out together and remain close to this day. My six "neighbor" cousins are much more like brothers and sisters than like cousins. We celebrated Christmas together, shared a single mailbox and a single subscription to The Daily Mining Journal newspaper. When Dad was ready to read the paper and it wasn't in the house, one of us kids was dispatched to fetch the paper from Bill and Jennie's place.

My little sisters, Susie, Kathy and Kelly are two, four, and six years younger than I am, and the next one older than me is six years older. My cousin Audrey is the youngest in their family and is a year younger than me, her brother Doug two years older than me and brother Rod two years older than Doug. It is this "gang of seven" that I associated with, in particular Rod and Doug, while the four "little girls" were very close, just as the "older girls" were.

Our neighborhood was full of kids. In the valley, the kids across the street from the Prusi homes were all at least six years older than me, but at the other end of the location there were quite a number of them close in age to me and younger. My folks had four kids in a fairly short span, then there was a six year hiatus, and four more of us came along in about a six year stretch. Bill and Jennie's six kids were similarly divided into the big and little kids. Of course the big kids in the neighborhood had an influence on us younger ones, especially the big sisters and older cousins.

Karen is the first born in our group and is one of the quieter ones. She is about fourteen years older than I am so I don't remember a lot about her while she lived at home. I remember when she went to work for the LS&I railroad though, and we got to go to the LS&I summer picnic as her guests. I also remember when she and Marvin got engaged. Carol is next in line, and I remember her babysitting us younger kids a lot. I don't remember when she let me roll off the bed while she should have been watching me. Evidently that made Dad kind of mad. She 'fessed up to this recently. I remember when she graduated from high school very clearly because I cried when I couldn't go to the ceremony with my folks and the older kids. Candy, I remember, as really enjoying the little kids. When she was learning to drive, Dad would let her practice on the valley road. We would play taxicab, and we kids would wait at the ends of the different driveways and she would stop and pick us up and drop us off at another spot of our choosing, knowing she would be back soon, and we could catch another ride. Cheryl is six years older than I am so we played the cool teenage girl and pesky little brother thing pretty much like you see it on TV. She had lots of friends over, and a lot of them were pretty girls, so I liked having her around.

Naomi (Mimi) is the oldest of Bill and Jennie's kids, and Kathleen (Punkin) is next. Each Christmas day all of us kids were back and forth between the houses, and I liked showing my toys to Mimi and Punkin because they always seemed so very impressed. I remember being in awe of Mimi because she went to college, and Rod and Doug told me about her college adventures and showed me the neat little NMU (Northern Michigan University) beanie cap she had. Punkin's husband, Chuck, brought golf to the neighborhood, and soon after he began coming around there was a four-hole course built in Bill and Jennie's yard. Chas was the first son of Bill and Jennie, and he is ten years older than I am. Naturally he fell into the hero role for his younger brothers and me. He was an outdoorsman and got to hunt with Dad and Bill, even going to the camp with them during deer season. He played football, and we admired his photo in the high school yearbook, lined up with the team in his uniform. He joined the army right after high school, and that sent his hero rating through the roof. When he was discharged and came home I think I drove him crazy asking him questions about army life and war games. Rod, Doug, and I were thrilled when he gave each of us one of his army shirts complete with the Prusi name tag and sergeant's stripes on them.

There were a lot of older boys in the neighborhood, and we younger boys followed their exploits closely. We envied them as they left their homes with shotguns in hand to go partridge hunting all by themselves, and we admired their cars when they acquired them. Chas was our connection to the adventures of the big boys, and these big kids introduced us to the adventure around Bellevue. One story is that of the swimming hole. One of the neighbor boys claimed ownership of it, I suppose because he was the first to swim there. My sister Candy bought it from him for a dime or maybe it was a nickel.

Most of the funny names we had for the landmarks in the area had to come from the older kids. But I remember naming one of them with my fellow little kids. It was up the road that ran between the bluffs, and it was another of the many rock outcrops that were everywhere. For whatever reason, this one caught our eye and lent itself well to being a play spot. We called it the Pirate Place. I think my co-discoverers were Doug, Audrey, Susie, and Kathy.

My first memories of our house are with it sided with some asphalt type of material with a fake brick pattern on it, sort of a tan color. The garage and sauna matched. Bill and Jennie had white wood siding on their house and black tarpaper on their garage. There was an old wood and wire fence around the two houses with small swinging gates for foot traffic and in our yard, a large gate that could be opened to allow a car to drive in. I was told a story by cousin Mimi about when Uncle Bill talked about painting or re-siding his house with my Pa, and Dad suggested he go with the same fake brick stuff we had on our house, to which Uncle Bill replied "Yuck." Perhaps this influenced Dad. Sometime during my early years, the house was re-sided. It was another asphalt type, green colored siding. The old wood and wire fence was also replaced with a white picket fence.

The borderline of Richmond Township and Negaunee Township apparently ran down the middle of the road that crossed the valley portion of Bellevue. The garbage on one side of the road was picked up by a Negaunee garbage truck. On our side of the road a truck from Palmer handled the chore. This was perhaps my first exposure to governments in action doing illogical things.

We went to grade school in Palmer till 1963 when I was in the fifth grade, and then all the grade school age kids in the neighborhood were switched to the Central Grade School in Negaunee. We had to make new friends in the new school and ride different buses. It was a big change. Not long after we made the change, the highway between Bellevue and Negaunee was closed, and now the trip to Negaunee had to be made via Palmer. Instead of three miles it was about fourteen. I think that was the beginning of the end of our days in Bellevue for it was only about two years later when all the families left the little valley and the small neighborhood just up the road. But that is another part of the story.

2

Life in the Valley

Our little home in the valley had to be pretty "cozy" when there were ten of us living there. Maybe the most we had there was nine, as my oldest sister Karen was almost twenty years old when the caboose, Kelly, came along. The two upstairs bedrooms were built such that the slope of the roof formed a good portion of the wall, so the beds were tucked under that. The bedroom occupancy was subject to seniority rules I guess, as the oldest resident kid seemed to have the plum spot. There was a crib in my folk's bedroom where the current infant slept. I don't remember too much about who was where at what time. For a while I remember my three younger sisters and I in one of the bedrooms with the older girls in the other. For a while I had the hallway to myself. That was my first opportunity to outfit a room of my own. Cheryl is the next child up the line in age from me, and she had the plum spot, the bedroom with the window that looked out at Bill and Jennie's house. There was a second story window on Bill and Jennie's house too, right across from the one on ours. I am told that for a while the "big girls" in the two houses had some sort of string and pulley system rigged up that they used to pass notes across with. Not sure what that accomplished that talking in a loud voice couldn't unless it was "secret" stuff, but kids like to do such things. Eventually Cheryl made her way out into the big wide world, and I moved into that room. Doug was then in the room across the way, and we were more technically advanced. We blinked signals at each other with flashlights. We didn't know Morse code or anything but we came up with our own series of blinks to represent words and had a blink vocabulary of about six words.

As mentioned earlier, there was no shower, and there was no real bathtub. We had that sauna out there attached to the garage. If I remember right, we had sauna on Saturday nights. The sauna is the traditional Finnish steam bath where a stove is fired to heat up a bushel or so of rocks atop the stove. Cold water is poured on the rocks to create the steam, and after a good sweat you wash up. I remember when I was pretty small and baths were needed but the sauna not heated, Mom and Dad would haul a big galvanized tub from the sauna into the kitchen and heat water for it. We had hot water in the house but I suppose the tank was too small to fill a tub. The water got heated on the stove, poured into the tub, and then the little kids piled in. The tub was set up near the stove, and the oven was on with the door open to help keep us warm. When we were done there were towels or blankets that had been warmed by the open oven door, and boy did it feel good to have one of these wrapped around you. My parents grew up in what you might call poor homes, and they had experienced the great depression during their first years of married life. As a result they were thrifty. That old tub had rusted through in a couple of spots, and Dad had just drilled the holes larger and put a bolt with a washer and rubber gasket through each hole then tightened a nut on each bolt to seal the leak. You watched where you sat when you got into that tub because the heads of the bolts didn't feel too great under your bottom. A weekly bath seems rather like we were savages now. Maybe we had sauna more than once a week. Maybe once a week was ok unless the dogs started to try rolling in us because we smelled so bad. Then I suppose the tub was brought into play. Often when the sauna was warmed there was company over to partake in that traditional Finnish bath and social event. Many of the aunts and uncles came over for sauna along with other friends of my parents.

On school days we walked the road up to the highway to catch the bus. Our dogs would follow us to say goodbye, and most days when we got off the bus after school the dogs were there, waiting for us. The walk down the hill often took a long while as there was no bus to catch, and kids can find so very many things to do on a short walk. Our mailboxes were here at the bus stop, and until the old woman in the farmhouse passed away, we made a habit of picking up her mail as we got off the bus. She said little when we knocked on the door but invited us in, thanked us, and presented some candy or a few pennies to each of us that had made the visit. I am not sure if she was just a quiet woman, or, like my own grandmothers, spoke little English.

There was one winter when the snow had a thick crust on it, and for several days we actually went to the bus stop early. We had found one of those temporary play bonanzas that Mother Nature sometimes bestows on lucky children. Beyond the highway was the railroad grade that had been built up. Its sides were steep slopes that were almost free of trees. We had taken to sliding down this slope with no sleds. We would just lay on our backs at the crest of the slope, push off and keep our legs up in the air and slide head first down the hill. The crusty snow made this possible, and my sister, Susie, had a coat made of really slippery material. She could slide faster than anyone else could. One time she had so much speed going that instead of coming to a stop at the normal place she slid on and down into the big gravel pit that lay between the highway and the tracks. I was watching from the top of the railroad grade and was amazed and frightened when just as she reached the rim of the pit and came almost to a stop, over the edge and out of sight she went. Fortunately this only resulted in an extended slide and no injuries.

On winter days when we got up for school, we ran downstairs and took up positions curled on the floor next to the heat registers. There were three of them, and these too were subject to seniority. One of them in the living room was the warmest, it being the closest to the furnace. It also was the spot where you could get heat on demand for when the furnace shut off and the fan quit blowing you could whack the wall there in a certain place and sometimes get the heat to kick right back on. Mom would bring us our breakfast there where we were curled up on the floor soaking up the heat.

It seems in the foggy recesses of my mind that one of my first memories is of standing in our yard early on a sunny summer morning and looking up toward the highway at the hills and forest. I can't even say for sure it is a memory but I think it is. It's a "feeling". Standing there with dew on the grass and the birds singing, and the morning sun feeling warm on me. The sunshine in the clear morning air gave the green trees a brilliance that struck even a little kid as being beautiful. I love mornings as much as I ever did, maybe more. Maybe I am blending the good feelings I have had on a thousand mornings into the pleasant peaceful memory of being a carefree boy. Whatever it is, it's a peaceful and pleasant thing to think about.

The little valley was picturesque to be sure, and for a kid it was a little bit of paradise. There were fields and hills and high rocky bluffs. We had names for the significant ones. Big Field and Twenty Clearing were, of course, fields. Step Rock, Slide Rock, and The Pirate Place were rocks down in the valley, the first two named for their shape. Cherokee and Wicked Apache were parts of the bluff as was The Bench where you could sit with a nice backrest and look down on the valley. I remember when I was too little to go "up the bluff" with the other kids, but stood in the yard and watched the small colorful dots that were the other kids climbing around on The Bench. How far away they seemed, and how I couldn't wait till I could join them on the bluff. I also remember when my sister Susie fell off the "high" side of Step Rock. We were playing there, and she sort of slipped and was hanging on with her arms and hands as her legs dangled down. Her eyes were wide, and suddenly she lost her grip and tumbled out of sight over the edge. Audrey and I were sure she was going to be badly hurt, but she wasn't. It's about a four foot drop so you get an idea how little we were.

It is amazing how kids can turn just about any place into a playground and any object into a toy. Those rocks were our jungle gyms. We had a large propane tank in the yard for our furnace fuel, and it was painted green. All of Dad's odds and ends were painted green. I suppose he got a deal on green paint one time. This tank served as all kinds of things. I think it was a dinosaur a few times, a stage for the performing arts and sometimes a boat or a rocket. It was used as a sort of chalkboard I guess because it was covered with initials and crudely drawn pictures scratched into the paint. I remember lying on top of it in the summer, and how warm it got from the sunshine. One of "the tank's" most memorable purposes though was as a racetrack or raceway. Spit races. We would lay on the tank and hawk one up and let it drop on the tank near the top, just off to one side where the curve started. The gob would begin to succumb to the effects of gravity and inch down, gaining speed as the curve got closer and closer to vertical. Once it reached the outward extreme it would drop off the tank into the grass, and hitting the grass first gave you and your sputum a win, leaving you jubilant and a small gleaming track running down the side of the tank, slowly shrinking and finally disappearing as it evaporated.

Just across the street from our house was our basketball court. The backboard was a round wooden wheel salvaged from one of the cable spools that the cable crew had abandoned when running the line from Negaunee to Palmer. It was fastened to one of the huge elm trees that lined our street. There was an electric pole near it that had one of our two streetlights on it. This allowed us to play basketball at all hours, and it was also the spot where we played our version of "Kick the Can". The way we played "Kick the Can" was to have a spot marked in the middle of the street for the can, and someone gave it a good kick. The person who was "it" had to run for the can and return it to its designated spot while the rest of the players scattered and hid. Once the can was back in place, the person who was "it" started to look for the others. I can't remember if you had to tag these people or just spot them to have them "caught". Once caught they had to come to the "jail" which was the big elm tree. There they sat till all were caught or until one of the others who were still free came along and gave the can another kick. That let everyone out of jail, and the search started all over again. This continued till all were caught, and the last one caught was "it" for the next round. It was just hide and seek with a can thrown in. We also played the regular hide and seek and another game where you threw a ball up on the house roof and called a name, and that person was it. The catch to this variation was that if the person whose name was called caught the ball before it hit the ground, he or she could throw it back up on the roof and call another name. You could only run until the ball was recovered, then the person who was it got to take a certain number of steps and toss the ball at one of the kids. If the person was hit they got a point, and if it was a miss the thrower got the point. After so many points you were out of the game.

 Usually we played these games in the evening, starting before sundown. The sound of our shouting and laughter filled the little neighborhood, mixing in with the clanking of the can as it got booted again and again down the gravel road. As the sun went down the sound of the frogs down in the crick would begin, and soon bats were darting around beneath the streetlight hunting for insects. We worried about them landing in our hair. I remember the chill starting to settle around us. With my memory being so full of those frog sounds and a chill, I think we must have done a lot of this playing in the springtime. No doubt the long winter had made us long to play these summer games, and once the ground was bare we couldn't wait to play "Kick the Can" again.

I don't remember playing basketball very much. We played some baseball, but it was hard to get enough kids together at one time for a baseball game. More often we played "five bucks up" where one of us hit the ball to a group of fielders. A one handed catch got you two bucks, a two handed catch one buck, and fielding a grounder got you fifty cents. If you made an error you lost that same amount. Once you got to five bucks it was your turn to bat. My Dad bought me a glove, and I remember he and I playing catch. Football is easier to play with a limited number of kids, and we played a lot of that, especially in the fall right after school. We didn't have any flat spots to play on. The best we could do was an open spot behind one of the neighbor's houses where there was just a gradual slope. Wayne and Kenny from the other end of Bellevue would come down and play with Rod, Doug, and me. There was a four-year age range in this group, and we littler ones took quite a pounding. You would cry for a while after a hard hit and get right back in the game.

I remember Rod giving me lots of encouragement and coaching. He told me what a good tackler I was, and I will never forget the time he told me I swung a bat exactly like Al Kaline of the Tigers. Kaline was my hero, along with Rocky Colavito. Besides having about the best baseball name of all time, Rocky Colavito was a real slugger and Kaline the complete baseball player. I remember watching Kaline on the Game of the Week one time, going into the bleachers to rob Mickey Mantle of the archenemy Yankees, of a home run. I took to doing my batting warm-up moves just the way Colavito did, holding the bat with a hand at each end and reaching it over my head and then down behind my back.

We must have made up a hundred different games, some of which were played for a day and others that sort of caught on with us. There was "Burpy" which was a game of tag, and the person who was "it" used a little toy machine gun—a burp gun—that made realistic machine gun noises, to tag the others. It was played around a certain group of cedar trees up on the hill. There was also "Feudin' Families", another gun game that Rod and Doug and I played which was simply running around, hiding, and pretending to shoot each other. When you got hit you threw yourself down in dramatic death throes, counted to fifty, and then came back to life to continue the feud.

The "crick" was a magnet, like all cricks are for kids. We caught pollywogs and frogs and minnows and mud puppies. We got wet and muddy. I remember Mom getting me a pair of rubber boots. "Swampers" is what we Yoopers called them. (A Yooper is a resident of Michigan's Upper Peninsula or U.P.) I had messed up so many pairs of shoes and socks with the muck from the crick that Mom bought the boots and set them right by the porch door. She told me I was free to go play at the crick but that I was to stop at the house and put on the rubber boots first. I know I tried to comply but sometimes when the mood to go "froggin'" hit me, I was so much closer to the crick than the house that I just couldn't delay my adventure by going back for a change of footgear. Poor Mom.

My parents, and of course Uncle Bill and Aunt Jennie, had been raised in homes where there was strict discipline. Both of my grandfathers were very stern men when they had young families to raise, which was pretty common in those times. They did not spare the rod. Dad used to tell about getting whippings when he stepped out of line. He also claimed that in the summer, he and his brothers got haircuts where their head was basically shaved except for a little knot of hair that was left for grandpa to grab hold of when he thought it necessary. Uncle Bill Ruuska, my Mom's brother, said that when grandpa Ruuska caught him or his brothers goofing off in the barn he was likely to get "one of those hair pulls when you could see all the windows at once". In spite of being brought up with that sort of discipline, my folks were a lot milder. I got spankings, slaps, and hair pulls to be sure, but I earned every one of them. Dad did all of the corporal punishment. I was not afraid of Dad, but had a healthy respect for the reach and method of his justice. That is as it should be. However, what was even more effective in keeping me on the straight and narrow during my teen years was the thought of disappointing my parents, especially Mom.

Another key player in my early years was one of the neighbor kids. He was six years older than I was, and he was one of those guys who seemed to have an interest in and a bit of knowledge about darn near everything. He was and (from what I hear) still is, what I would call a "Yooper Intellectual". The Yooper Intellectual is someone who is intelligent and well read, capable of great things. He (or she) is also in love with life in Upper Michigan and is unlikely to leave. The Yooper Intellectual usually never goes to college and works in one of the mines. Doug and I followed our resident YI around like puppy dogs. We were like the mad scientist with his two flunky assistants. We learned about astronomy and dinosaurs and microbiology. He had a microscope, and with it we looked at pond water and saw it teeming with strange life forms. With his microscope had come a dissecting kit. I won't say much about that other than to say that to the local frogs, our YI was the equivalent of the Nazi, Doctor Joseph Mengeles. This fellow seemed to always be reading something scientific, and he would get so enthusiastic about what he had learned that he just had to share it. Doug and I soaked it up, and I have to say that his enthusiasm was such that it was hard *not* to be interested. He should have been a professor, and I think of him as one. The Professor was involved in many of my adventures.

My oldest sisters and cousins began leaving home when I was pretty small. Some of the girls had moved to the "big city" of Minneapolis, Minnesota. Cheryl became an airline stewardess for a while. These days they are "Flight Attendants". When they came home to visit it was exciting, and we got to go to visit them at their new homes as well, sometimes staying with them for a week or so in the summer. What an amazing place that was for us! I got to go to a Minnesota Twins game at the old Met Stadium one time with Dad and some of the husbands of my older sisters and cousins. We saw a couple of young boys catch foul balls with their gloves, and I was sorry I had not brought mine. The excitement of the ballpark and seeing famous athletes was quite an event for me.

Then the weddings started. They were such big family events even for us littler ones. We had other cousins whose big brothers and sisters were getting married too, and we boys took to seeing who could eat the most ham buns at a wedding. I can remember when my oldest sister Karen and her fiancé Marvin came home and told the folks they were engaged. I remember Candy getting married at the house, and most of all I remember when Cousin Naomi got hitched because it was the first wedding I ever participated in. Her sister Audrey and I were both red-haired and freckle-faced, and some people thought we were twins. So Naomi had us serve as the ring bearer and flower girl. I am sure we were adorable but what I remember most was that my suit coat had an inside pocket, and in it I "packed" a toy snub-nosed 38 throughout the wedding. Right after the ceremony I showed Rod and Doug, and they got a big kick out of me packing heat at their sisters wedding.

Of course then the babies started coming along. I became an uncle when I was about seven or eight years old, which I thought was quite unique. We had brothers-in-law and nieces and nephews, and it seems there was plenty of love to go around. Each addition to the family was an exciting event.

Such was the flavor of life in our little valley.

3

Young Legs

The energy of youngsters is something to behold, and the kids from Bellevue had their share. I am sure that when the weather was bad and we couldn't be banished to the outdoors we had to have driven Mom about over the edge. Dad worked shifts at the mine, so he often had to catch up on his sleep during the time when we were all awake. We loved to play outside, and no doubt we were sent outside even on the rare days when we didn't want to be. I don't remember ever being told to stay in the yard or to not go far. I am sure we were told such things when we were small, and I am sure that some of the older ones were given the responsibility of making sure we followed orders. But we were given freedom to roam at a very young age, and roam we did. We had the curiosity that all kids have and the young legs to take us where we wanted to go. In my own case, when I read or heard about things, it made me want to see or do the things I had learned about. Besides emulating the heroes of the books I read I wanted to see things like giant water beetles and mosquito wigglers and flying squirrels. So much of the wonder of childhood is that just about everything is brand new! Finding your first mess of frog eggs or a shed snakeskin when you are five or six years old is exciting stuff. I learned about mosquito wigglers from the Professor, and I didn't quite believe him when he told me they breathed through their tail, so I went and found some in a pond and watched them, and by golly he was right. If you are lucky, you keep this curiosity with you throughout life.

We explored the woods and the bluffs and of course the crick. I don't remember ever worrying about getting lost. Sometimes it was just Doug and I, sometimes other lads and sometimes, big groups of boys and girls. We went on picnics and "roasts". A roast was when you brought food that had to be cooked and you built a fire. This usually consisted of potatoes and marshmallows. The potatoes were put to bake in the coals of the fire and left there while we went off and played for a while. We would come back and fish the potatoes out with sticks, all black and ashy on the outside. We cut them open and put butter and salt on them. Naturally there was a good supply of black ash mixed in but man they were tasty! The marshmallows I remember were purchased in little packages made for a roast. There were about six or eight of them in two rows in a box with a cellophane top. We didn't get to bring "pop" (which is what we called soda) on our picnics, we got Kool-Aid. It was usually in an old jelly or other type of jar with a piece of waxed paper placed between the lid and the neck to keep it from leaking. Peanut butter sandwiches were the usual main course. We also "foraged" on what Mother Nature provided. Pin cherries, choke cherries and fall cherries, strawberries, hazelnuts, raspberries, and black berries. There were even these little tart tasting leaves that grew close to the ground that we ate. In the late summer and fall there were apples. It seemed that there were wild apple trees everywhere. Many an adventure was temporarily paused to fill up on apples or one of these other treats. Sometimes we couldn't wait for the apples to ripen and ate them when they were still rather like wood. Mom warned us not to because one of our cousins had "almost died" from eating green apples. We picked them for Mom to make pie, and one time I remember that I offered to go pick a mess of apples for her if she would make one pie just for me and she agreed. I loved that apple pie. The black berry patch up near the railroad tracks was terrific. I have never found a better one; in fact I have never found black berries in the area where I live now. We don't have the apple trees either, and I miss being able to stop during a grouse hunt to sample a wild apple from a tree growing in the middle of nowhere.

The bluff that was beyond the hill behind Bill and Jennie's place was quite a playground. There was actually a trail that continued on past the gravel road that ended at the last driveway in the valley. This trail led between two bluffs. Our "main" bluff was on the right side of this trail, and by following the trail you could get to the "easy way" up the bluff. Taking the easy way you just had to climb a very steep hill. This route was also one of our favorite places for "parachute rides". We would shinny up skinny saplings on the side of the hill, and when we got to the whippy top, we would throw our weight towards the downhill side and hang on. The tree would start to bend over and give you a slow ride down to the ground, actually below where the tree was rooted. Slow if you chose a tree that was matched properly to your weight. Too thick and you didn't go down. Too thin and the treetop would break off, and down you went like a meteor with a small tree growing out of your hands. We learned that maples were less likely to break off than poplar.

When we got "older" we turned our noses up at the easy way and took the hard way up the front of the bluff that faced the houses. You had to do a bit of real rock climbing on this route, and as we got older yet, we explored different routes along this face of the outcrop. We had a few hairy trips while trying this. Along this side of the bluff down at its base was the "landslide". Sometime long before, a portion of the bluff had broken away, and a large field of boulders covered the slope. It was hard to walk over and a great place to hunt for porcupines that liked to use the spaces between the rocks for dens and hiding places. There was a really neat formation on the front of the bluff that we called "Cherokee". It was a small flat rock shaped sort of like an arrowhead pointing out away from the face of the bluff. It was a nice place to sit and look down on the landslide and the forest around it.

If you climbed the hills on the other side of the valley beyond the railroad tracks there was the old pastureland from that dairy farm. There was a spring in the middle of this pasture. Just a small hole in the ground, perhaps twenty feet across with clear cold water bubbling up out of the ground and running out a small outlet on the downhill side of the hole. It was full of interesting life forms, a great place for catching frogs and pollywogs. On one of our first expeditions there, we were amazed to see a brook trout darting around the pool! We managed to catch it with our hands, and I think it was a twelve-incher, which was a real trophy for us. We found out later that my cousin Chas and his pals had put a bunch of trout that they caught in the crick into the spring after transporting them "overland".

Beyond the pasture the hills were covered with hardwood forest. Old farm sites, trails, and railroad grades could be found here. We explored them all. There were two ancient railroad trestles that crossed ravines. The tracks were long gone from the grade but the trestles remained, and I remember the day we got brave and crossed both of them. Part way across one of them the trestle swayed a good bit, but it didn't collapse, and we made it across. We would make a habit of rapping on dead trees or wiggling them. Sometimes even knocking them down just to see if anything was inside of them, and many a time we chased flying squirrels out of these den trees. One time a few of our friends from town were with us on an expedition, and we almost lost one of them over the edge of the bluff. Then as we rambled around I found a newborn fawn, curled up and hiding. Actually, I almost crawled on top of it as I was on hands and knees going through the forest. How beautiful it was there. One of my town boy pals suggested we kill it but I must have had a little of the conservationist or sportsman or human in me already because we vetoed that plan and got quickly away from the little deer. I knew Dad would be happy with me for making that decision.

Many of these adventures were unplanned. We followed our noses and went where they led us. What started out as a roast could end up with parachute riding or squirrel tree shaking or porcupine hunting. We were adaptable and energetic. One evening, the Professor wanted to go see the new highway that was being built. It was the new M35 that would make the trip from Palmer to Negaunee about ten miles instead of six and replace "our" highway just up the hill from us. Doug and I were all for taking a look. It was nearly dark or maybe already dark when we set out. We followed the trail between the bluffs that went through "Big Field" and hit the new road right-of-way. It was still under construction. We thought it was cool to have this big new road all to ourselves so we walked it all the way to Palmer, then back home along the old road. It had to have been at least a six-mile walk, and I remember it being a wonderful lark on a beautiful evening. The cool of the night refreshed us, and the stars in the sky were something to behold.

Another marathon walkabout occurred when Doug and I had one of his school pals from Palmer around. This lad claimed to have seen girly magazines and said they were pretty darn fun. Naturally we were interested. How might we get a look at these things? Well, he said there were a few places he knew of where we could see them. All of these places were in Palmer though, three miles away. Three miles was no barrier to us so we said, "Let's go!" and off we went. It seems his first surefire stash of girly pictures was empty so we continued to another spot that was also empty. But he "knew" that we could find them out at the Beagle Club outside of Palmer so off we went there. It was no short jaunt, and when we got there, there were no pictures of naked girls to be found at all. I think now that this guy was just pretending he had seen pictures of naked girls, and we sort of forced him into a corner. I think he kept leading us around hoping we would tire of the pursuit. Fat chance of that. We were country boys who walked everywhere, and now we had real motivation! At any rate, we never found our girly magazines and just had to walk all the way back home. That was just as well. Maybe someday I will see such things but I don't really care anymore.

I only remember one time being concerned about finding our way home. On that occasion we *wanted* to get lost. Cousin Rod and the Professor had once been lost when I was real little. They spent a night in the woods, and the police and the men from the neighborhood were searching all night for them. They got home a little scared and cold but with no other ill effects. Of course they were heroes to Doug and me. One summer Doug told me that he and I were the same ages that Rod and the Professor had been when they got lost and thought we should have an adventure like that. So off we went into the woods, hoping to get lost. We took off in a direction we hadn't explored much and just wandered and wandered. Unfortunately after hours of wandering and not being real sure where we were we came out on the Rolling Mill road and knew exactly where we were. It would be too much work to start trying to get lost again, so late in the day so we hoofed it home.

Young legs also get the itch to run away sometimes. What kid hasn't run away? Our attempt to get lost doesn't count as a runaway attempt because we hoped that we would get rescued and return as heroes like Rod had done. But there were other attempts.

Doug and I had found a great place to play over behind the Professor's garage. An old wooden boat was leaning against the back of the garage, and we could slip behind it and hide. It was such a great hideout that we thought we should run away to it the next morning. We would get up extra early and sneak off to the hideout and stay there all day and make the folk' search for us. What fun that would be!

The next morning I awoke very early and stealthily dressed and stole out of the house. A nice summer morning with dew on the grass is what I remember. I went over to Doug's and waited for him but he wasn't coming out. I waited and waited and finally realized he was sleeping, and I would have to go in and wake him up. Doors were never locked in those days, and it wasn't like it was a problem for me to walk into Bill and Jennie's place because we never knocked ever. It was like part of our own house and the kids all came and went in both houses whenever they chose. I just didn't want anyone to see us make our exit. So I was pretty sneaky and made it up to Doug's room where he was sawing logs to beat sixty. It seemed strange to be moving around the house with everyone asleep. I tried to quietly wake him but couldn't, so then I tried a little less quietly, and that didn't work either. Finally I heard someone moving around outside the room, and there was Auntie Jennie standing in the doorway.

"Danny! What are you doing here so early?" she asked. She wasn't angry, just surprised. I said I was just trying to get Dougie up to come out and play. She told me it was too early and to come back later. I left and decided I would have to go it alone. I got over to the hideout and crawled in. It would still be fun. Maybe it would even be more fun because when they started to look for me Doug would know what was up, and he could sneak over to keep me posted on the search and tell me how worried Mom and the girls were. Yeah it would be more fun that way.

Time passed pretty slowly under that boat. I hadn't brought anything to play with. If Doug had been there we could have chuckled over how clever we were and had a high old time, but of course he was still snoozing and the search wasn't getting off the ground too quickly. Maybe I shouldn't have started quite so early. Soon time quit going slowly. It just quit going. I was bored silly. I should have brought one of those "Gameboy" toys with me. Too bad the "Gameboy" was still about forty years away from reality. It turned out like most runaway attempts do. Before anyone even missed me I had had it with life on the run, and I abandoned the plan and went home. I'm not even sure if anyone was awake when I got there.

My next attempt went a lot better. It was many years later. I was probably in about third grade or so when life at home got to be just too much. My folks loved my sisters a lot more than they loved me and treated them a whole lot better. They probably wouldn't even miss me if I ran away for a whole day. So one morning I did the early rise thing again. My plans were a lot more ambitious this time though, and I would go it alone. I grabbed up my little dime bank that Auntie Jennie had given me for my birthday the year before. It was a little metal cash register, silver colored. It only accepted dimes, and when you put one in and pressed a lever it swallowed up the dime. Right where real cash registers have numbers so did this one, and it showed you how much money was in the bank. The bank would automatically open when you got ten dollars worth of dimes into it, and on the day I made my break it was at seven dollars and something. With my life savings in hand, I struck out for Palmer.

On the way to the big city as I walked along the road and down a hill I heard crashing in the brush alongside the road. Whatever it was it was coming towards me. It had to be a bear or a pack of wolves! As the critter got almost to the right-of-way opening I could see the brush moving as it ran quickly and noisily along, now turning to go parallel with the road. I started to walk faster, and I remember trying to control my fear and not run back home! The critter moved along with me for several yards and then turned and headed back towards where it had come, never giving me a look at it. That had been a close one, and I was proud that I was brave enough to keep on heading to Palmer instead of turning around and going home.

I am sure I tried thumbing a ride but didn't get picked up and ended up walking the whole way. Somewhere along the way I broke into my bank, destroying it in the process but now I had seventy plus dimes jingling in my pocket, and it felt pretty darn good. I walked to my friend Jimmy's house, and he was surprised to see me as we didn't often see each other during summer vacation. I took him aside and told him I had left home. I had left home, and I was never going back. He laughed! I convinced him I was serious and he agreed to let me hide out at his place. What a fun day we had! We hit the IGA store and loaded up on candy and bought some toys. I think I blew the whole wad. I remember buying a set of plastic racecars. They were all shaped the same but in many different colors, and there were ten or a dozen of them. We had some great races that day. I also got a taste of what it was like to live in town, going everywhere with Jimmy and playing with our other school friends. I had a lot of fun. So much so that running away felt pretty darn good. I think I even forgot that I was a man on the run.

Towards afternoon, Jimmy's mom said that my folks had called looking for me. They had been worried and were coming to get me. This was working out pretty well. I had not been lonesome yet, and I had not had to figure out where I would spend my first night on the road. My folks appeared to be sufficiently chastened in that they had worried about me. Soon they arrived to take me home. I thanked Jimmy and the folks thanked his mom. My Mom got on my case a little bit until I told her why I had been forced to take this drastic step. She was sympathetic, or at least knew she had to pretend to be because I seemed so serious. Pa didn't say much at all. I think Mom had *suggested* to him that he not say much. I returned home to a newly appreciative family, and the only thing it had cost me was my life savings and a good sunburn. I found out on the way home that I was not the only one to "break the bank" that day, as someone had robbed the bank in Palmer while I was there. They probably went straight to the IGA store with their loot so I was lucky I got those racecars when I did.

I have a couple of interesting post scripts to these runaway stories. In about 1971, Doug was living in Minneapolis, and I was in town to visit him and other family there. Another friend and I were out with pals and they dropped us off at Doug's apartment where we were supposed to stay. It was late, after midnight I am sure, and Doug was sleeping. We rang the door buzzer for a long time. We pounded on the window for a long time, and then we went to a pay phone and called him, and I let the phone ring one hundred rings. He never woke up, and we had to call someone to come and pick us up from a gas station near Doug's place. If you plan to do anything with Doug, schedule it for the middle of the day.

In 1996 I attended my 25th class reunion in Negaunee. My wife and I were mingling with my old crowd when across the room I spotted Jimmy, the friend who hid me out that day in Palmer. We walked over to him, and when he saw me coming he smiled and laughed and we shook hands and said hello. We introduced our wives, and as soon as that was done he turned to his wife and pointed to me and laughing said to her, "This is the guy who ran away to my house." She knew the story already, and we had a good laugh over it. Apparently Jimmy had enjoyed my adventure as much as I had.

4

Mentoring

There are ads on television now where famous people do public service announcements encouraging us to do "mentoring" with young folks, to help them grow up to be better people. I guess it's good to remind folks about doing that because we can forget that every kid doesn't have a full quota of mentors. For myself and for my siblings, that was never a problem. I don't know if everyone would agree that I turned out OK, but so far I haven't done anything worthy of a prison sentence. It would appear that my wife and kids love me, and my dogs even seem happy when I return to the house after work each day. Whatever the end result of my upbringing, it was not negatively influenced by a lack of mentors.

My cousins, Doug, Rod and Chas, are all like brothers to me. (I did get shortchanged pretty badly in the biological brother department). Of the three, Doug is the closest in age to me and was my best friend. The other two were my "big" brothers. I looked up to them, and both have helped me learn things about guns and the woods and fishing and maybe even girls. Perhaps they got me in a little trouble too now and again, but the net effect was positive. Uncles Charley, one on Mom's side and one on Dad's, also were good to me and gave me examples of how an older man should help a younger one. (I just realized that 75% of the mentors in this paragraph so far are named Charles. Perhaps I should have named one of my sons Charley.) As I grew into manhood, mentors continued to pop up when and where I needed them. I have been fortunate to have many older men who helped to guide me.

Like most of us, my Mom and Dad were the keystones of my mentoring. They raised eight of us with love, patience, and understanding. Dad worked in the mines, hating it (I found out later) but doing what he had to do to keep food on the table. Layoffs and strikes were frequent, just as they are now for the men in the iron mines. It could not have been easy for them, yet they hung together and cared for us, and the financial hardships didn't spawn bickering or abuse as they do in some families. We just didn't get out for ice cream cones as often as most kids do today. Our household had one car, one phone, one TV, usually one to three dogs, and 10 people that loved each other.

Mom is one of the kindest people I know. She has a tough time speaking ill of anyone, and if someone else does she often will take the side of the person who is being criticized. She is and was an old-fashioned mom and grandma. She cooked and cleaned, didn't drive, and loved her kids like only a mom can. She made great bakery. I have vivid memories of Saturdays when I was a preschooler. I got to sit and watch cartoons with my younger sisters while the rest of the house was a whirlwind of activity. My older sisters had to clean the house with Mom, and Mom always baked. The smell of their cleaning concoctions and baking caramel biscuits and saffron bread filled the little house. Mom could make things right when they were going wrong. Everyone knows a hug from mom makes skinned knees or bee stings feel much better. Remember getting hugged by your Mom? It has a special feeling and I doubt that anyone is ever comforted so much by another person as a child is by his or her mother.

 Dad was (of course) my hero. He was a real outdoorsman and included me as much as he could from the time when I was little. He loved brook trout fishing and also fishing the spring run rainbow trout out of Lake Superior. He took a weeklong vacation every year to deer hunt and hunted grouse and rabbits as well. By the time I was old enough to hunt he was about 50 years old and had slowed down a lot. He used to hunt ducks and keep rabbit hounds and also trapped a little, but that was before I came along. He was a very quiet man, not given to "chatter" about things. Cousin Chas told me Dad was smart, because he didn't talk much and nobody ever learned anything when they were talking. If you follow that line of reasoning, that puts Chas and I among the dumbest men alive. Dad liked to read though he didn't get much time for it and he had been a pretty good fast pitch softball player when fast pitch was the hot sport for young men. People around Negaunee often commented to me about the old Negaunee Township ball teams that were pretty much all Prusi boys. Dad had eight brothers.

 There was no public library in Palmer, where I had been schooled for my first several years, and getting to Negaunee from where we lived wasn't one of my regular activities. I remember when I started getting bussed to school in Negaunee, one of the first things I did was get a library card, and for a long time I read a new book each night. Most were outdoors or history type books, and Dad would often pick them up and read them as well. We had the same taste in literature. In fact, Dad named me after a famous man from history, who also was quite a hunter, that being Mr. Daniel Boone.

 One of my favorite outings with Dad was a fishing trip to Black River. Black River is the township where my Mom grew up, about thirty miles from where we lived. The folks lived there with my grandparents for a little while, and Dad loved the area enough to buy a little piece of ground and build a hunting shack there. During the annual maintenance shutdown at the mine, Dad always got two weeks off, and we would move to the "camp".

Our fishing excursions to *the* Black River usually started from the camp, where the whole family had spent the night. About 4 AM Dad and I got up and had our breakfast of crispy fried eggs and bacon. Mom and my sisters would sometimes stir when they heard us and smelled the breakfast cooking, but realizing the time of day would just roll over and go back to sleep. These were wonderful outings; the memories are vivid. The new sunrise sparkled the heavy dew as we drove a short hop to my cousin Nancy's place, where we parked the Plymouth in her yard. Dad would do his routine of slipping out of his shoes and into his hip boots, and pulling on his old, olive drab army surplus coat that held all the odds and ends that fishermen seem to need. Being a small boy, my gear consisted of the rod and reel and a pair of rubber boots. All I had to do to be ready to go was pick up my rod, so I always stood patiently and watched dad prepare and admired all that neat gear, dreaming of the day I would have such treasures. I remember the old steel bait can with a piece of electrical cord forming the strap that went over his shoulder and the landing net. That old army jacket seemed to have a hundred pockets, and each pocket held some little piece of equipment. Then there was the wicker creel. Later if we were lucky, I would watch Dad line that creel with several handfuls of green grass pulled up by hand and slippery with dew, to cradle a fresh caught brook trout. The brooks were beautiful with their colorful speckling and hooked jaws. It was a thrill for a young boy to see the colorful fish wiggling on its new, unwelcome bed of grass as the morning sunshine warmed us on the riverbank.

After the preparation ritual it was off to the stream. Dad's strides seemed to equal about four of mine, and the wet ferns and grass had me soaking wet before we were even close to the stream. The new summer day was being welcomed by a thousand singing birds, and if it was early enough in the season, the drumming of the grouse. I remember one trip where Dad stopped suddenly and pointed out a saw whet owl perched on the shaded limb of a balsam tree, staring at us from only a few feet away. If we got to deep water that needed crossing, I climbed on Dad's back for a horse ride across. I have never felt as safe or as secure as when I was riding on my father's back, holding onto his wide strong shoulders as his long strides carried us towards our destination.

When we got to the river, we always fished side by side for a while, and then we would split up. When I was very young, Dad would usually set me up at a good hole with a supply of night crawlers and work his way along the stream. When I got older, we would strike off in opposite directions on the river. We usually caught some trout. Never a big pile of them, but usually enough for a meal. After four or five hours, Dad would decide we could call it a day and it was back to the car. Once there, I always hoped Nancy would spot us because if she did she always asked us in for coffee and goodies. I liked the goodies. I don't remember what Nancy's specialty was, but I remember being anxious to get into her kitchen.

Black River Location was full of our relatives, (still is I guess) and my hunting and fishing trips with Pa usually involved a visit at Jake and Irene's, George and Fanny's, Mart and Shards, or any one of a half dozen other relative's homes. Visiting was still big entertainment in those days, and the Finnish people, which we are, like to converse over coffee and "dunks". All my aunts could bake very well, and I took full advantage of their skill and hospitality.

Anyway, I started out talking about mentoring. The things I just wrote about didn't mention a lot of instruction that I was given by my mentors. Rather it shows the importance of just treating the young folks well so that they learn about respect for others and about sharing your time and your love and your knowledge with them. Dad never gave me many "on the road of life, there are many strange turns" type of lectures, but he taught me about being a dad just by really being one. Unfortunately, I lost him when I was seventeen and just getting to the age where we had begun to talk to each other on more of a man to man basis. Mom gave a little bit more advice, but mostly showed all of us how much devotion and love for people can accomplish. She also showed how much easier it is to get along with people if you and that person will have a mutual acceptance of the other in spite of any faults that exist. Mom is still with me and still practices her unconditional love.

Judging from how my sisters turned out, I would say they had pretty good parenting. First and foremost it came from our Mom and Dad, but the parenting chore is something that aunts and uncles and other influential adults all take part in. Most importantly, our parents stuck together. It's too bad that every child doesn't have such an expanded circle of "parents". If they did, we wouldn't need public service ads to encourage mentoring.

5

Prusi and Prusi—*WORMS*

My cousin Rod and I were once trading stories about the adventures of parenting. Rod's middle two children are boys that are pretty much the same age as my two sons. These four boys are young men now. Three have a child of their own, and the fourth is about to be married. All four spent time searching for that personal niche of theirs, with varying degrees of success. All are good decent young men whose only real problems seemed to be the innocence of youth. Rod put this into words very well.

"Kids" he said, "Figure that the world should fall into place to accommodate their plans and when it doesn't, they just can't understand why."

That, in a nutshell, describes the one big drawback to being young. When you get older, you may still make big plans for your life, but if they don't pan out it isn't quite as much of a surprise to you. All of my life, I have fallen victim to a kind of cockeyed optimism with regards to making my hobbies pay off financially.

When I first got into raising beagles, I thought I could sell lots of registered pups and make all kinds of money. It didn't quite work out that way. Likewise when I tried raising game birds. I wanted very much for the bird business to become a way to make some extra cash doing something I really like. Twenty years ago, just the fact that I wanted it badly would have convinced me it would happen. By the time I took up the bird business, I realized it probably wouldn't, and if it had, it would have been due to hard work and some good luck, rather than just by me wanting it to happen. The only thing that wanting it badly is good for is to keep you enthusiastic about sticking with the work. I remember well the first such undertaking that I was a part of, and it was Rod and I who launched that enterprise.

I was probably eight or ten years old, so Rod would have been twelve or fourteen. Summer vacation had just liberated us from the bonds of academia, and we had three months of unencumbered adventure to look forward to. Country kids like us didn't get to town a lot, and most of our activities didn't cost anything. Still, we were always wishing we had some money to spend. Neither of our families was very well off. I would pick "struggling" as the best word to describe the economic station of the Bill and Walt Prusi families.

We had one set of neighbors across the street who, to me, always seemed to be a bit better off than the rest of the families in our end of Bellevue. The kids were older than we were, and it seemed that they had pretty nice toys, and when these kids began driving they seemed to get their own set of wheels shortly thereafter. Now it may be that this was just a perception on my part, the old "grass is always greener" syndrome, but it was my impression at the time.

The two sons in this family were young entrepreneurs. They sold worms. I still remember the nice sign they had up on the highway. It was three wooden fish silhouettes, hanging from a horizontal bracket of sorts. Each fish was hung by screw eyes from the one above it. The top fish said "WORMS". The lower two said "Angle" and "Dew" respectively. It was a nice little sign that I thought very clever. The going price was two cents for a dew worm and one cent for an angleworm.

All of what I just told you about the neighbor kids is what got me sucked into the big worm venture that summer. I can't take credit for the idea, for that was all Rod's, but I did jump in with both feet when it was presented to me. I suppose I had visions of my own sign up on the highway with bigger fish and fancier writing than the one the neighbor kids had. Rod spelled out the plan as follows.

We would dig a thousand worms. Yup, a thousand. We would transport them via bicycle to the bait shop in town. There we would sell them to the bait dealer for two cents each, split the loot, pocket ten dollars each and be rich. Easy as that. Ten dollars went a long way in the early sixties. Especially if you were a kid who usually never had enough money to carry it in paper form. I agreed instantly to Rod's proposal, and we got out our shovel and went to work.

Things were not planned very well, but all the talk about having ten bucks interfered with what little ability we had to reason or think things out. We could have called the bait shop to see if they needed worms. We could have asked what they would pay us for them if they did need them. Logic to a youngster though, needlessly clutters up your lovely ideas. It has happened to me in my forties, no reason it wouldn't happen to me when my age was still in the single digits.

It took us two or three days, maybe more. It was sunny and hot, and we dug in unbroken ground. We had to break sod and turn it over and bust it up to find the worms. I got pretty worn out, and Rod ended up doing most of the hard work. He didn't get mad at me for it, he just did it, and he still planned to split the cash fifty-fifty.

I don't remember any of the other kids being around to comment on our project. I really can't remember that we were doing this in secret but we may have been. Or, the other kids thought we were nuts for working so hard when we could be catching frogs or trout or building tree forts. I don't remember any comment from the folks either. Maybe they were pleased to see us out trying to earn our way in the cruel world.

I think we ended up stopping at eight hundred worms. Eight bucks would be good enough, or maybe we would just dig some more worms later. We would go to the bait shop with our eight hundred worms, collect our cash and promise the old guy that ran the place that we could get plenty more.

We headed into Negaunee with our squiggly treasure. Rod rode his bike and I think I walked part of the time and rode on his handle bars part of the time. I didn't have my own bike then, but that would sure change when this worm business took off. It was about three miles in to town. When we got to the sport shop, Rod did the talking.

Old man "Boosta" ran the sport shop. It may have belonged to his kid, but he was always the guy behind the counter. He was elderly, or it seemed to me he was. He had lots of stories and always took time to talk to us kids when we came in to the store. He knew we seldom bought anything and that we were just there to gawk at all the wonderful tools of the hunter and fisherman. He would do a trick for us where he would pull on the loose skin of his Adam's apple and pop out his dentures. I will never forget his reaction that day when the two bumpkins walked in to sell him eight hundred worms on the spot and bring him two hundred more later.

"A thousand worms . . . . " he said softly, looking first at one of us then the other.

"A thousand worms . . . . " he repeated. He glanced out the window, then back at us. He lifted his cap and scratched his head a little and glanced out the window again.

"A thousand worms for twenty dollars . . . . " and shook his head.

Boosta let us down easy. I suppose he realized that we had put a lot of work into getting these worms and didn't want us to have done it for nothing. He had no need for a thousand worms, he told us, as gently as he could. The worms we had were almost all angleworms, not the big night crawlers that most of the fisherman wanted. He sold angleworms for a penny a piece, so he sure couldn't give us two cents each for them.

At the time I was pretty mad, and I thought that he took advantage of us. He gave us two or three bucks for three hundred or so worms. When I think of it now, I'm sure he had no need at all for our worms, but wanted us to get something for the work we did. It was really nice of him to do that, and I was just too young to realize it and not a little frustrated that reality was putting the kibosh to my wonderful plans. We headed for home with our few dollars and most of our worms. I was crushed. We had a plan and a good one, but the world didn't fall into step with it. How dare it! Rod was positive about the whole deal. Maybe he was trying to cheer me up, I don't know, but he seemed as though it didn't bother him at all even though he had done most of the work.

This is another one of those examples of how older ones can do good for the younger ones. Boosta was kind to us. Rod was positive and did more than his share of the work. It didn't dawn on me then, but it has come to make a lasting impression on me.

Now I wonder if I could get Rod to go partners with me on raising birds? Maybe we could drive a truckload of them to Michigan and see if Old Man Boosta is still around.

6

Boy's Best Friend

In my nearly fifty years of life, there have been only a few of those years when I did not have one or more dogs. I have three right now and have often had four or five. The most that ever lived with me? Fifteen, but that was when one of our four dogs had ten puppies, and then a stray showed up that we took in for just a few days. You either like dogs or you don't, and I obviously like them both as hunting companions and just plain companions. The first of "my" dogs were Speck and Jip. Mom had always told me they were mine, and they were the same age as me. If I remember correctly they were pups of my Dad's hunting hound Bugle Ann, and they were born under a porch. I don't remember a whole lot about them, as I was awfully small. Jip got killed by the school bus. It happened up by the railroad crossing, and I remember being in the car and driving by and peeking out at him lying there. I was too little to really feel sad. What I remember is he looked like a black and tan pancake. Speck was around for a while longer. He was pretty lame from having been caught in a leghold trap. Dad finally had him put down, and I remember crying about that. One of the older neighbor kids told me about it (rather gleefully as I recall) and it hurt. This happened in the late fifties, and back then when you put a dog down you didn't bring him to a vet. You did it yourself or had a friend or neighbor do it if you couldn't bring yourself to. Man and dog went for a walk and only man came back. This might sound cruel, but I don't see it as being any crueler than having the vet do it for you. Would you rather go for a pleasant walk and have the lights go out suddenly or be brought to a strange place with strange smells and strange people all around with glum faces and be injected with something? The 1950's Bellevue way was probably kinder.

After Speck and Jip, there was a steady parade of dogs. Mostly they were mongrels. Blackie and Corkie were cocker spaniels. One of them liked to tear my pant legs and chew on my toys. Then there was Jingles. None of these were around long or made much of an impression. But then came two dogs that all of us kids remember. Smokey and Tramp.

There was a peddler that came around every now and again. An old fashioned door to door salesman. He had a huge trunk full of all kinds of wares, and Mom and Aunt Jennie were pretty good customers. On one of his visits he brought along a litter of puppies that he said were water spaniels. He was selling them and Doug wanted one, and by golly his folks bought him one! This was pretty remarkable, paying real money for a dog. I have seen water spaniels since and also many pictures of them, and Smokey didn't look like any of what I have seen. He had colors like a beagle and hair like a cocker. He was built low to the ground and stocky. He was a good dog. Even-tempered and he learned to run rabbits as good as any beagle could. He was mild around people but fearless if he got into a scrap with another dog. One time he and another dog got into a real serious battle, and Doug waded in to break it up and was bitten in the process. The other dog got the blame but I witnessed that melee, and it was such a blur of fur, teeth and boy that I am not sure which dog drew blood on Doug. He might have bitten himself.

A year or two after Smokey came along I was wanting a dog. This may have been around the time my youngest sister Kelly was born but I think it was after that. When the folks called home from the hospital to announce Kelly's birth, I started bawling when I heard it was another girl, and I really wanted a brother. I was put on the phone with Mom, and she told me I could get a puppy. I quit crying right away. I could probably put up with new *twin* sisters if I got a dog out of the deal. At any rate we called about a litter of pups somewhere off towards Marquette and went to look at them. I picked out one of the squirming fur balls and took him home. He was a mutt, all black except for a white patch on his chest. I can't actually remember how excited I felt but just two weeks ago I picked up a new golden retriever puppy. The feelings I had then were familiar and made me feel like a kid, so I imagine the new puppy feeling is something that remains constant for dog lovers throughout their lifetime.

Tramp grew up to be bigger than Smokey. I would say he was fifty pounds or so, and Smokey was thirty-five or forty. Tramp was rather tall and lanky as opposed to the short and stocky Smokey, who taught Tramp to run rabbits. What adventures the four of us had, Doug and I and those two dogs!

The dogs often walked us to the bus stop and met us there when we returned from school. They came along with us on our travels through hill and dale. They chased rabbits and cars and fought with the neighbor dogs. A Volkswagen hit tramp one time but it only gave him a bloody nose and confused him for a while. I'm not sure how the beetle came out of it. One time the dogs went missing for a while, and we were up at the other end of Bellevue playing with the kids there, when running down the railroad tracks, and out of the mine came a whole pack of dogs, Tramp and Smokey right in with them. They were running with the pack. Not a good thing, but we all make our little ventures into the wild side when we are young.

Tramp was good-natured too. He never bit anyone but he would bark and growl a bit. In fact, when we were at school and Dad at work, he would guard Mom. When she was home alone and Tramp was in the porch he would stand in the doorway and growl menacingly at anyone who came over. Mom would have to put him in the basement or something if she wanted to let the person in. I don't know if Tramp would have bitten someone if they tried to get past him, but nobody tried. But he was basically gentle, for when we kids would tussle around and wrestle; if ever one of us pinned another down Tramp would get involved and firmly but gently pull whoever was on top away from the other.

These two dogs had been around for several years when we added two more pups to the family. Duke was a hound pup. All ears. He was beagle, bluetick, and Walker hound. Dad got him in hopes of turning him into a rabbit hound. Then we got Beauduy, who was a sort of beagleish mongrel. One of my sisters got him from some family friends named Beauduy so that's what we called him. I was dog wealthy now! These newcomers joined in our adventures.

That spring I roamed the hills and fields of Bellevue with my three dogs, and often Smokey as well. Sometimes with Doug but often alone except for the dogs. I had a little store-bought fiberglass bow and a half dozen store bought arrows. The dogs and I would strike out after school or on the weekends looking for adventure. Those spring days in school get awfully long, and when I got off of the school bus, I ran down the hill, wolfed down supper, changed my clothes and was gone. I don't remember a lot of dangerous or exciting encounters by adult standards, but we got a chipmunk once and shot it out with a skunk one day right at dusk. It was a running fight led by Mr. Skunk with me at the end of the line and Beauduy, Duke, and Tramp in the middle. The skunk and I would stop every few yards and take a shot at each other. The skunk and I emerged unscathed but winded. My three dogs all took direct hits from our striped foe. It would have been interesting to see how my mother would have reacted if I had been hit.

Another time I was on my bike cruising around with Duke trotting along behind. The snow banks were still three feet high along the road where the winter snowplowing had packed them and piled up the snow. We rode over to the upper end of Bellevue a half mile away to see if any of my pals were out and about. Before I could find any of the neighbor kids, we ran into trouble. A couple of big dogs owned by people up at that end of Bellevue were out in a field looking for who knows what and they spotted me. They charged us from a hundred yards away, snarling and barking as they came, and I goosed that Huffy like my life depended on it. My attackers couldn't see Duke because the banks hid his small frame from their view, and of course he couldn't see them. He DID hear them coming, and the fighting instinct of his bear hunting ancestors kicked in. He charged for the growling sounds that were coming our way. He zipped up the snow bank and came nose to nose with one of the timber wolf wannabe's which was a big white German shepherd type. Duke went for him growling, and the big dog was so surprised by the sudden appearance of this spunky pup that it turned tail and ran! I watched as I pedaled, calling desperately for Duke thinking it was only a matter of time till the big dog realized he was being chased by a puppy. Then Ole Duke would be lunch for the pair. The shepherd was bookin' for the hills, looking behind him at his pursuer, and he ran right off the edge of the bank where a driveway cut through it, smacking into a parked car with a loud bang.

About this time I had to turn my attention to the other dog, this one a regular old German shepherd, who had glanced at the predicament his partner was in and chose to kill me while his pal distracted my bodyguard. I was pedaling hard, going uphill, and the growling mutt was gaining. I pulled my BB pistol from my belt and shot him in the chest—I think—and pedaled some more. He flinched a little but kept coming. I turned again and shot with the same result. This sequence repeated itself about four more times, with no real change in the situation except the dog gained a little every time I quit pedaling to turn and shoot. Finally as I topped the hill, he just gave up on me. My guess is he just got to the border of what he considered his turf and decided he was satisfied to have us leave. As I holstered my trusty (but impotent) shootin' iron, little Duke was suddenly running alongside of me. He looked happy! I know he was thinking, "*Man*, we kicked their *ass*!"

My three dogs and I parted ways when we left Bellevue, and I don't know what became of them, but Smokey moved to Black River with Bill and Jennie and lived a long life. I hunted rabbits with him there many times. I remember a story Uncle Bill told about Smokey that happened long after the move.

Uncle Bill had been very ill with heart problems, and his doctor told him to get regular exercise by walking. He was trying to do this even though it was difficult for him. Smokey wasn't too active anymore either at this stage. One evening they took a walk behind their house along the dirt road to Perna's lake, and as they walked along together, Bill noticed one of Smokey's sworn enemies, a rabbit, sitting alongside the road. He walked a little further towards the rabbit and then stopped and watched Smokey to see if he would see the bunny. The rabbit got nervous (perhaps recognizing Smokey) and took off at a run right down the road away from them. Smokey saw the rabbit and took off like a rocket, baying his rabbit hunting battle cry. Bill said it was incredible how the old and crippled dog came to life at the sight of that rabbit. Off went the rabbit with Smokey in hot pursuit. Uncle Bill stood and watched, and the chase went out of sight around a turn in the road. Then suddenly Smokey's voice stopped. Bill walked after them, worried what he would find around the corner. He said he thought Smokey might have died of a heart attack. When he got around the corner, there was Smokey, leaning on a tree trying to catch his breath. The rabbit was forgotten.

Smokey and Tramp are gone from this earth but not from our memories. I don't believe that animals have souls, so I don't believe they go to heaven. But they live on in our fond reflections on the time we spent with them. They enrich our lives while they are with us and long after they are gone.

7

The Best Pond Ever

There are people who have accused me of having a somewhat unnatural (and perhaps unhealthy) affection for ponds. I have been digging holes and letting them fill up with water for years now. Had I not figured out long ago how to make other people pay for them, this could be a serious problem. But given that the various public and private agencies that look out for wildlife think I am good at digging holes that fill with water and have been generous with their funding, it's only a minor eccentricity.

A few years back I was working on one of my pond projects with the help of my boys. I think the boys still resent me for making them put in so much time working on my hobbies. Perhaps I did too much of this, but at least I never beat them.

Anyway . . . .

We were building a dike of sandbags to plug a ditch. We were yacking away and somehow got to talking about me and my pond building obsession. I had never really put this all together before that day, but as I told my history to the boys, it became clear to me that this attraction must have started in the womb or shortly thereafter.

Environmentalists keep telling us how wetlands are fascinating and diverse ecosystems. They don't have to tell that to kids, which I guess, tells me that grownups know less than kids do in some areas. All young boys and most young girls (especially those from Bellevue) like splashing in puddles and looking at the bugs and crawly things that live in ponds and cricks. You start out splashing puddles, move on to noticing things that live in puddles and ponds and cricks, then on to catching those things. It's only natural that you would progress to creating puddles and ponds and cricks. Right?

I remember when we were in grade school, and we would walk down the hill from the bus stop in the springtime. The snow would be melting, and little rivulets of the melt water would run down the edges of the road from the bus stop down to the crick. Of course, the water was orange because our soil was rich in iron ore. Sometimes that hundred-yard walk from the bus to the house took two hours because there is nothing like water and mud and sticky snow to distract a young country boy from anything else that might be on his agenda. The sticky snow was used to construct dams. We would pick up a double handful or two and plop it down in the path of one of these little rivulets of orange water. The size of the reservoir we could make depended on how many dam builders we had and how big that trickle of water was. It would always end up as a race. We would lengthen the dam as the size of the pool increased; and of course had to add to the height of it as well. We made a lot of trips to the snow bank as the horseshoe shaped dam grew and grew. We had to "pank" the snow of course. Using our boots, we firmed up the snow enough to hold the water. The upstream edges of the dam would begin to turn orange as the water soaked in. Sometimes we got ambitious and began building more dams upstream till we had a series of them. Then we would stand below the uppermost of them in the now dry channel, place our boot on the upstream side of it and drag our heel through the dam releasing the flood. The orange water would race through, washing the gap larger and larger, and as the wall of water (all of six inches tall) swept downhill it would take out the downstream dams as it went. Great fun. (This was before Play Station.)

In the summer time, we spent a lot of time at the crick. We took to damming up the crick just about every summer too, trying to make a pool large enough to float a raft. I remember very clearly one time when the older kids had dammed up the crick and built a raft and were going to see how far upstream they could sail on it. Somehow I missed the big launching, and I was too young to join the adventurers, but I remember running down to the bridge. The great unknown had already swallowed up the raft full of explorers. I could hear them laughing and talking but they were out of sight, and it seemed like they must have been at the very edge of the known world.

As I got older, I was able to build my own rafts and play a major role in dam construction. In fact, I bet it was one of my dams that was the best engineered, best built, that Bellevue ever saw, and it resulted in the best pond ever. Doug was involved, and I think the Professor may have been as well. When things went wrong, the Professor usually had a part in it.

It was dam building time that year, which is to say it was a time when we thought a dam would be fun. Coincidentally, Dad had tossed out one of those wooden lattice type things that you have on the sauna floor to keep your feet off the concrete. It was of a perfect size to lay across the two cement culverts that ran under the road down at the crick. We put the wooden lattice across the upstream side of the culverts, and the current held it there. The fact that there was current enough to hold it tells me the water was running pretty well, and it was probably early in the summer or late in the spring. We then found a large sheet of tin that was the same size as the lattice and put that against the lattice as the major barrier to the water. Then we cut sod and built the remainder of the dam out of it. Can you imagine that? We cut the sod into rectangles and laid it there all across the tin, piling it up till it was about three feet tall and even with the top of the tin. This was a well-built dam. It was strong, and it allowed very little water to seep through. In fact, once the water got up to the top of the dam, there wasn't much of an opening left in the culverts to carry away the overflow. We didn't see that as a problem.

The best pond ever began to form, and we had rafts built and sailing in no time. In just a day or two we could sail rafts farther upstream than I had ever seen anyone sail, and the water still hadn't reached the top of the dam. We were making history. Then Ma Nature got involved.

During the night, it started to rain. This would have been about the second or third night of our dam's existence. We were snug in our beds. No doubt I was dreaming of exploring the uppermost regions of the crick on my raft the next day. Boy did it rain. I mean I never heard it or saw it, but man it had to have really rained.

One of the neighbors came home from work late that night. When he drove down the road, as he got near the bridge, he found that the road was under water. He could not drive across. I would say that about a hundred yards or so of the road was inundated. He had seen the handiwork of the dam builders over the last couple of days so he knew who to get on the phone with. My Dad got a late night call from a rather agitated fellow who wanted to get home to his bed. Dad had to put on his waders and go down to the crick in the middle of the night, wielding a large crowbar and destroy our beautifully engineered and constructed dam. Boy, I wish I could have watched that wall of water when it let loose! I wonder if any homes down steam were swept away. I remember Mom giving me a little lecture the next morning. Dad was at work already and by the time I saw him he wasn't all that mad. He was probably impressed at the quality of our dam. After all, he DID get to watch the wall of water sweep downstream when he wrecked the dam.

FAMILY PHOTO ALBUM

The valley as viewed from "The Bench" atop the bluff. Bill and Jennie's white house is in the foreground. Walt and Hilda's is barely visible behind it.

Newlyweds Walt and Hilda Prusi (author's parents) at their first home in Negaunee in 1937.

A young Bill and Jennie Prusi in front of her parents home about 1939.

Walt and Hilda's oldest three girls, left to right: Karen, Carol, and Candy.

The big girls when they were little. Left to right: Karen and Naomi (back row) Carol and Kathleen (middle) Candy (front). Naomi and Kathleen are better known as Mimi and Punkin.

An early vacation trip for Walt and Hilda with their first four girls. Left to right: Hilda, Cheryl, Karen, Candy, with Carol standing behind.

The Walt Prusi's in 1960. Back row left to right: Karen, Carol, Candy, and Cheryl. Front row: Kathy, Hilda, Dan, Kelly, and Walt. Sue is on the back of the couch, obviously having a good time.

The Bill Prusi's with their youngest four. Left to right: Rod, Bill, Audrey, Jennie, and Doug, with Chas standing behind.

Hero and worshipper. Walt and Dan.

Kathy poses on the slide, 1960. The tank and rocks behind it got far more use than the slide.

Rod, Dan, and Doug, all dressed up for church.

The "little kids" show off their Christmas "name gifts" in 1963. Back row left to right: Doug, Dan, and Rod. Front row: Kathy, Kelly, Sue, and Audrey. Nephew Kevin Koukkari sits in front of Sue.

All dolled and duded up for the 1965 Negaunee Centennial. Left to right: Kathy, Audrey, Dan, Sue, and Kelly. The garage and sauna are to the left and some of the neighbor's homes and the big elm trees can be seen in the background.

Audrey, Kelly, Sue, and Kathy take on the leaves in 1961.

Left to right: Doug, Audrey, niece Bridgette Kovala, Sue, and Dan. Rod is atop the tank holding niece Wendy Kovala. The boys are all "packin' heat".

Left to right: Kelly, Dan, Kathy, and Sue. This photo was likely taken the year the family moved away from Bellevue Location.

Left to right: Ben, Danny, and Tara, the author's children in 1985, another generation of country boys and girl.

The author with his grandson, Connor, in 2001. The ATV is quite a step up from a "carboggan", but country boys will always be country boys.

The author in 1961, obviously an untroubled country boy.

8

Snow Day

Every Yooper kid and I suppose every kid who lives in snow country, knows the wonderful feeling of being awakened during the night before a school day by the sounds of howling winds. Snug and warm in your bed you know that a blizzard is raging outside and hope, eternal hope, fills your spirit. Maybe, just maybe, Mother Nature is gonna write you a pass from the world of academia. It's hard to get back to sleep but you are smiling as you try. You drift in and out of slumber. Finally you hear Mom up and around, and you can tell that she is listening to the radio. You want to just pull those covers over your head and sleep some more, but you don't dare let yourself until you get the official word. Sometimes it's late in coming, and you have to get up and go through the motions of preparation, and sometimes you just can't believe it that you actually have to go to school in such conditions. Once or twice we were actually on the bus when the word came through. Better late than never, but the sweetest thing on those mornings is when you never have to leave the snug confines of your covers because Mom hollers up the stairs,

"*No school today!*"

The warmth of your blankets is now matched by a warm feeling inside of you. Finally you can let yourself relax and sleep in. But not too long! Snow days are way too fun to be spent indoors!

An unexpected day off is just so much fun for a kid. You are so full of good feelings that you even consider playing with your sisters. You laughed at your school clothes as you rummaged for your "snow pants" and mittens and "wooly socks". If Rod and Doug didn't call me or run over, I would be calling them or running over. Sometimes the storm was just too severe at the moment to actually have fun outside, and if that was the case, I would be over at my cousins or they would be over at my place. Most often the girls would be at one place and the boys the other. I said you would consider playing with your sisters. You weren't often forced into actually doing it. We had plenty of toys and games and good imaginations if we had to stay inside, but most often we braved the elements.

We would bundle up so that we looked like small but colorful Michelin Men. I remember how when you stepped outside, the wind and snow would hit you in the face and take your breath away. It was a shock at first but you got used to it quickly. It was just plain fun to be out in that storm. We tunneled and we built snow forts. We found steep banks that had drifted overhangs of snow near the top and would jump into these to break them loose and make mini avalanches that carried us along to the bottom of the slope. We found high places with deep drifts below them that we could jump off of into the fluffy cold snow. These high places sometimes included the houses. We would find sheltered spots or dig them in the drifts and hunker down. It was fun to be out of the wind and hear it roaring over your little burrow. Fun to be warm in a snow bank while it was cold outside.

Achilles had that heel, and I had my wrists. It seemed like my mittens and my sleeves just did not get along and kept trying to keep distance between each other. The warmth of the exposed skin would melt some of the snow, and that water would start to freeze on my cuffs, and soon my wrists were being scratched and frost bitten at the same time. I remember how red they got and how they burned. I stuck it out as long as I could. When we had had enough and headed inside, there was usually a plan in place to warm up and then get together for some indoor play. Occasionally we had so much fun outside that we would just go in for a warm up period, and then do the outside thing all over again.

The warm up thing was great. Mom would often have the stove on with its door open for us to warm ourselves. Snowy and/or wet socks and mitts and scarves were hung around the stove or heat registers while we had our hot chocolate and toast.

The aftermath of a blizzard was almost as good as the storm itself. No skier ever loved fresh deep powder as much as we did. We had to explore the neighborhood to see where the big drifts were so that we could tunnel into them. There might be a new and undiscovered avalanche-making place. The plows may have created a huge snow pile somewhere that would be a good fort site. One glorious winter we had three consecutive snow days.

As we grew older, the outside play was not as interesting to us as sleeping in. Actually just getting out of class was pretty hard to beat. It was when I was in junior high that we once created our own snow day.

It was a snowy day but not so much so that school was in jeopardy. As always, the bus picked us up as its first passengers of the day. The route took us through Palmer and out on a dead end road that reached several miles out of town. We picked up kids from one or two houses there, and then it was back to Palmer where the bus filled up, then it was on to Negaunee and school. On this particular day, when we got out to the end of that dead end road, the bus turnaround was not very well plowed out. Our driver was having a difficult time getting the huge yellow beast pointed back towards Palmer, and he asked for some assistance from some of the boys. He asked them to go to the back of the bus and look out and direct him when to stop as he backed up so that his wheels wouldn't drop off the road into the snow filled ditch. Several volunteers moved to the rear seats to help. As he backed up, the boy or boys shouted, "Keep coming . . . yer ok. Keep coming . . . " till, with a thump, the rear wheels of the bus dropped into the ditch. "OK STOP!" said one of the smiling lads in the rear seats. Mr. Bus Driver was rather upset. He called us inconsiderate. I have to admit that he was right. I am not sure who was the mastermind of this deception or who carried it out. Rod would know.

The bus driver had to go to the nearest house and call the school to tell them his pride and joy, the yellow behemoth, was mired in the snow and out of action. He then prevailed upon some of the folks who lived there to transport his hooligan passengers to Palmer where the school said we would be able to catch one of the many other buses that would be running through town. We caught our ride to Palmer and were dropped off where we normally picked up our big load of Palmer kids. They were gone, I believe having already caught another bus. There must have been a half dozen or more of us Bellevue kids in this gang, and we had some vague instructions that we were to hook up with one of the other buses. Had our instructions been more specific maybe we would have made at least some token effort to comply, but what we did was immediately go into escape and evasion mode. When we saw a bus headed one way we headed the other. If one came down the street towards us we took off down a perpendicular street and ducked into the first alley. It was like a scene right out of a comedy show. Even the girls, who normally would have nothing to do with such a scheme, got caught up in the fun of hiding from the buses. There were several high school buses that passed through Palmer, and then the grade school bus runs started immediately afterwards. We managed to miss all of them. Finally when no more school bus traffic could be seen, someone called the school and told them we missed all the buses. I believe the person at the school was a bit agitated but asked if we could find a way home. This turned out to be remarkably easy, and soon we were enjoying a snow day. Mother Nature helped with this one, but she only scored an assist.

9

Ragamuffin Sniper

Confession, they say, is good for the soul. Confronting painful memories from our past and addressing them, they say, is good for our mental health. These theories I now put to the test.

I am and have always been, what one might call overly sensitive. Little things that happen to me often bother me a lot more than they should. I wish it wasn't so, but that is me and I have learned to live with it. The story you are about to read is a sordid tale from my past. It describes an incident that I am not proud of, and because of my shame I have, for many years, avoided speaking or thinking of it.

My healing began when I first saw "A Christmas Story" on television just a year or two ago. For those who are not familiar, it is a story of a young boy and his efforts to convince his parents to get him a Red Ryder BB gun for Christmas. It's a wonderful story that captures beautifully the psyche of a young boy. For me it was a walk back in time.

I think it was when I was about nine or ten that my heart became set on a BB gun. My cousins Rod and Doug had them, and they were allowed to "pack heat" at will when they roamed the woods and fields around our homes. I was no stranger to shooting, as I had been shooting a 22 rifle under Dad's supervision since I was about four years old. But I didn't have that BB gun that was actually mine and available to use whenever the mood struck. I don't remember much about my campaign to get the BB gun. I know that I said that I wanted one for Christmas, and I got the standard line much like the one the mom in the movie used. The "putting your eye out" possibility was brought up, and unfortunately backed up with the true story of one of my cousins losing an eye to a BB. But the next Christmas there was my BB gun under the tree. My sisters will tell you that I don't remember my campaign to get the gun because I was spoiled and got whatever I asked for. They are probably right too.

The gun was so cool. It wasn't a Red Ryder, but it did have a "fake" exposed hammer for looks, and I think it even had a saddle ring. It was a little more fancy than the ones that Rod and Doug had, but all were Daisy brand. It came with a little container of oil and a tube of copper BB's and instructions on care and maintenance. Of course, I had to show it to Rod and Doug at the powwow we held each Christmas day to check out each other's haul of gifts. Rod, I remember, was very impressed and told me what a good BB gun I had.

I know that during that winter I peppered a lot of tin cans and such, and in the spring I was afield with my new weapon but I don't remember being out with it that often. Maybe my gun privileges were limited, I don't recall. I am sure that I thought I would be bagging a lot of chipmunks and squirrels and birds with my new gun. I had been working my way upward with my weaponry. I started by chucking rocks at critters, moved on to making slingshots and then got a bow and arrows. I was never too successful at taking "game" with any of those and as it turned out I was pretty inept with the BB gun as well. This pattern of ineptitude has continued throughout my life.

It was a beautiful spring day. Maybe it was summer. All I remember is that it was nice out, and sunny. I was hunting around the yard with my BB gun, and throughout the day I had heard shouting and fun going on in the woods up on "the hill". I wasn't exactly sure who it was but later in the day down the hill came Rod, Doug, and our cousin Wally. They were all armed with their BB guns, and when we saw each other we naturally joined forces. I don't remember exactly all the things we did. I suppose we hunted birds and chippies and such as we wandered here and there. We found ourselves up on "the highway" and beyond. Most likely, we were headed for an old railroad grade near an abandoned farm that was known for its excellent chippie hunting. Somewhere along the way somebody got the bright idea that we should try for bigger game. Automobiles were what they had in mind.

Whenever you watch a movie or TV show that feature a gang of bad guys, the gang consists of a standard list of characters. There is a leader. There is a real "bad dude". Occasionally the leader and the "bad dude" are the same person. Then there is the schmuck. There may be more characters in such a gang but these three are essential. The schmuck is always the first guy to get killed or captured. Half the time, the schmuck gets killed by his own gang. Standard procedure is for the "bad dude" to kill the schmuck under orders from the leader. On the day I am describing, I was no older than ten years old. I know this because by the time I was eleven the highway had become a dead end with nothing but local traffic to our houses in the valley below. But on this day the highway was a target rich environment. If I was ten, Rod would have been fourteen and Doug twelve. I think Wally is Rod's age. Now that you know the ages of our band, you have a pretty good idea, which of us was the schmuck. Doug may have been considered a schmuck too; I'll let you be the judge of

Country Boy

that. Rod was probably the leader. Wally may have been the leader but he was definitely the bad dude. Shooting at cars was something that the rest of us might have done on our own, but I had the impression that it was the kind of thing that Wally did all the time. I am sure he fueled our sense of adventure and exploited the dark side of Rod and Doug. Schmucks just go along. Now I am not saying I was forced to take part in this. I am sure I was happy to walk on the wild side under the protective umbrella of my "gang".

We took up positions in a stand of saplings below the highway grade and alongside of it. We cocked the guns and waited. Cars began passing by, and we would shoot at them. Soon someone scored a hit . . . DOINK. We all laughed. We began getting creative and rolling several BB's down the gun barrels so that when we shot it had a shotgun effect. We got more hits, and more evil laughter echoed through our leafy hideout. The traffic began to increase. The shift change at the mines was about to happen, and there were a lot of miners that traveled this road. I can still remember feeling scared but exhilarated, and when one of the gang laughed, I laughed too and soon I was not very nervous at all. I should have been.

I think the car was red. There were four or five guys in it on their way home from work. It passed by and we scored one or more hits. We got distracted by other targets I suppose, and didn't think much about it when this red car now came into view again going in the opposite direction. We let him have it again. Baaaaaad move. The tires squealed as the driver stood on the brakes. As I type this I can remember the feeling of dread that filled me when I heard those shrieking tires. The doors of the car flew open and it seemed like forty guys jumped out. They all looked seven feet tall and the slowest moved with the speed of an Olympic sprinter. I think we all froze for a second. I know I did. Then we bolted. I would bet that the four of us hit speeds in our first few strides that we have seldom if ever matched. I saw Wally leaping over some obstruction, a log I suppose. He flew threw the air, his arms out like wings, his BB gun flailing. I remember the sunshine hitting his blonde hair. I caught glimpses of

Rod and Doug but they were just blurs in the brush. I think someone had hollered something but I don't know who it was or what he said. It was probably something useful like "RUN"!

As I ran, my mind was filled with dread. Branches whipped my face, and I caromed off small saplings. I ran for all a ten-year old is worth, and I could hear my companions crashing through the brush off to the side and ahead of me. They were all faster than me!

My heart was pounding, as much from fear as exertion. I was coming to the edge of the stand of thick saplings and would soon be in more open woods where I could reach greater speed. There was a fleeting moment of euphoria when I realized that, and my mind began a debate. Hide or run? It was a fleeting moment. Both the debate and the euphoria ended when I heard brush crashing and feet pounding behind me. One of them had me in his sights!

Just as I emerged into the more open area I caught my foot and went nose-diving into the leaves of the forest floor. My ankle hurt, and the pounding footsteps were upon me in a heartbeat! My rifle was pulled from my hands, and I covered my head and started bawling. My pursuer ran on past me towards the sound of my fleeing companions. I looked up and saw the man's face. It scared me. He paused for a second and now held my gun in both hands. I screamed!

"DON'T SHOOT 'EM MISTER!"

What the heck was I thinking? I would have been happy to take a BB in the ass over being in the fix I was in, and I'm sure my gang would rather have been shot at then caught as well!

"I just might!" growled back the seven-foot tall ogre.

He gave up the pursuit and came back over to me and grabbed my arm, jerking me to my feet. I wailed like a banshee. I had no idea if he was gonna beat me to death with my own gun or just stomp me. Instead he headed back for the highway, dragging me along as I sobbed loudly. When we got out into the open, I could see the rest of the guys from the car pool emerging from the woods and coming to the car. They shouted a bit to each other that they hadn't caught anyone. I think I was happy for a second that none of my partners had been caught. Then I realized

I would be the sole object of attention for all these pissed off miners. When the others saw that their friend had captured me, they all came over and it seemed like they were all chewing me out. There were four of five of them.

They showed me a dent in their car where one of our BB's had taken off some paint, and they chewed me out. They told me that if I had hit a window it would have shattered, and they might have crashed their car. They said I could have blinded one of them. They bitched and they yelled and I cried and I cried. They all got in the car and sat me between two of them in the front seat, and said they were taking me to the cops.

My wailing was done but I still sobbed. I thought to myself how I should not have let the "big kids" talk me into this, but of course I had not complained about the plan. I wished I were faster. I lamented the fact that I hadn't run towards the highway and hidden in the culvert that ran beneath the road. They may not have seen me and if they had, I could have held them off with my trusty BB gun till the cavalry came to my rescue, not thinking that the cavalry would have been on their side. My trusty BB gun. It was now in the hands of one of these very angry men.

My pain was immense. I wanted to die. My Mom was gonna cry and my Dad would probably never acknowledge me as his son again for the great shame I had brought upon him. I was a bad kid. A really, really bad kid. My captors cooled off a little and stopped yelling. They asked who I was and I told them. They asked who my Dad was and I told them. They knew my Dad. Terrific!

At the Negaunee Police Station I was brought before a very serious looking cop and sat down in a chair. My tormentors told him what had happened, and Mr. Cop began to question me, and I started bawling again. He grew angry and I wondered what he would do. A captured soldier should only give name, rank, and serial number and never give out information that would possibly harm his comrades. A CIA spy would suffer torture rather than admit that he was a covert soldier of democracy. They could torture me or they could kill me. Maybe that would be best . . . just killing me. No, I thought . . . they're not gonna do that. Probably they won't even hit me. I was still scared silly. But these weren't the Russians and I wasn't a gallant soldier fighting evil forces. I was a crook! A vandal! One of the Bad Guys! In a heartbeat, I turned State's Evidence. I sang like a canary. I named the names and pointed the finger. I spilled it all and named the parents and where they lived, and if I had known any of their shoe sizes or birthdays I would have told them that too. The cop wrote it all down. When we were done he turned me back over to the miners and asked them to bring me home, but he took the BB gun.

The men brought me home and they had softened. They were actually quite nice to me. They didn't come in the house and talk to my folks. I guess they figured I had been through an ordeal and my folks would likely put me through another one. When I think of it now, they were very kind on that ride home. What's the point of taunting a man on death row?

For the life of me, I can't remember much about what the folks said or did to me. When Dad got home from work he growled at me about the "stunt" I had pulled. I know that the cops called or visited Wally's folks and maybe called Rod and Doug's folks. They all kept their BB guns hid for a while. I don't think the car owner asked for any money to fix his car. Nobody got sued or went to prison. Rod and Doug never got mad at me for spilling my guts that I remember, and although Wally made some noise about beating me up he never mentioned it the next time I saw him. But I never got my BB gun back. I am pretty sure that Dad could have gotten it back from the cops had he wanted to, but I suppose he felt losing my rifle would teach me something. I have often wondered if it lies rusting in the basement of the Negaunee Police Station.

Everyone has pivotal moments in their lives that can alter their course. An event or a person turns them from good to bad or bad to good. So did this terrifying experience put me on the straight and narrow? Come on . . . I was ten years old. I still pulled stunts. I was just sneakier, smarter, and faster. And I learned to keep my mouth shut.

10

Yodskof Space Capsule

Kids everywhere learn early about vehicles and locomotion. Babies get little walkers and then it's Kiddy Cars and tricycles and bikes and sleds and toboggans and the whole series of things that meet the human need for increased speed and increase the human need for the medical profession. We were no different. A lot of the kids in the neighborhood enjoyed skiing and ice-skating but I never got into either. All of us liked sleds and toboggans, and we did plenty of riding on those. In Bellevue we came up with a couple of vehicles that I think were unique.

The first was the "carboggan". The name came from the Professor, our resident Yooper Intellectual. The vehicle itself came from Uncle Bill's '64 Chevy.

Uncle Bill had sort of a freak accident that could have been serious but ended up only being an expense. He had been driving along the highway when the hood of his car opened up. Evidently it wasn't latched or the latch broke, and the wind got under it and pulled it open. Of course he couldn't see out of the windshield and had to look out the side window and guide himself to the shoulder of the road. Luckily nobody was hurt, as he had to have been going fairly fast. The hood buckled and had to be replaced. This worked to the benefit of the ragamuffins.

We turned the hood upside down and jumped on it to straighten it out as best we could. It wasn't exactly smooth but we got it almost back to its old shape. We fastened some rope to it and dragged it up the hill by Bill and Jennie's house. It was wintertime and the hood became the "carboggan" and it was the most unique snow vehicle we had ever had. It wasn't fast, in fact till you got a trail packed it was really slow. But once you got a packed trail for it to glide on, it would get you down the hill reasonably quickly. It was heavy and a real chore to get back up the hill but you could fit a half dozen of us on the thing, and all those kids could get it back up the hill when they all pulled on the rope. Because it was heavy and bulky, once it got moving down the hill it didn't steer at all and nothing short of a sizeable tree or rock was gonna stop it. Fortunately it never met a sizeable tree or rock. It was also fortunate that none of us kids got in front of it or we would have become part of the packed trail. The carboggan was not used for very long. The novelty wore off as dragging it up hill was . . . well it was a drag. Not so with the Yodskof space capsule. After its inception it never lost its charm, and I've never heard of anyone besides us coming up with such a creation.

Cable TV was coming into being, and a cable company was running line from Negaunee to Palmer. The cable was brought in on huge wooden spools. The "wheel" portions of the spools were four or five feet in diameter. The center hub was hollow. Many of these empty spools were left alongside the highway once the cable that they had held was installed, and not a few of them found their way into our possession. We tried using them for various forms of entertainment, and through trial and error and inventiveness, the Yodskof was born.

We came up with the idea of sawing a hole into one wheel to

gain entry into the hub portion. It was named for a Russian space vehicle, real or imagined I don't really know. A cosmonaut kid could climb into the hub and be rolled around by his pals or down one of the many hills. It was a thing of beauty. I remember one of the first test flights.

We wheeled the capsule part way up the hill behind Bill and Jennie's. I don't recall for sure who got the honor of being the test pilot but I think it was the Professor or maybe Doug. We had a launch crew who would hold it in position till the cosmonaut got inside. Then we had the safety crew, which consisted of two "stoppers", me being the second. If I recall correctly, the first of the stoppers was part way down the hill, and he was to slow the vehicle if it got moving too fast. I was sort of the emergency stopper. I was down in the yard, and I had an old discarded automobile steering wheel that had the steel rod of the steering column attached to it. I planted myself squarely in the intended path of the capsule and rammed that steel rod down into the ground. I held the wheel between the Yodskof and me and braced myself. The idea was for me to stop the capsule in its tracks if it got that far. I was on flat ground, and we thought that if it got to me at all it would not be moving too fast.

With our test pilot inside, the launch crew sent him on his way. Things looked A-Okay. Capsule speed began to increase rapidly. The first stopper attempted to slow the vehicle but failed. Velocity increased. It kept increasing. We were losing control of the situation. I was the last line of defense and looked across that steering wheel at this wooden comet hurtling down upon me. When the Yodskof hit the flat spot in the yard it didn't slow down one wit, and as it bore down on me, discretion won out over valor, and I abandoned my post. The hub of the thing hit dead center on the steering wheel and pushed it right over. The wheels straddled the steering wheel and the hub rode over it causing the wheels to leave the ground till the hub cleared and then the whole thing came down with a thump. This slowed it down a bit which was fortunate for the next thing it hit was Auntie Jennie's clothesline pole, and that thing wasn't going anywhere. With a loud bang the Yodskof re-entered the atmosphere.

I caught some flak for not sticking with my post but it was a small price to pay for escaping uninjured. With this flight under our belts we began to fine tune launch and flight procedures. We learned the best way to brace yourself inside so that you traveled round and round with the rotation as opposed to bouncing around. We learned to fly with two and even three (if they were small) cosmonauts inside. We even got confident enough to take flights without a launch crew. This was accomplished with the use of a board that you propped against one wheel holding the capsule in place on an incline. Then you got inside and sort of rocked the vehicle till the board fell out, and gravity did the rest. This ended in near disaster for Doug and me one time.

We were doing a double cosmonaut run with no launch crew, and all went well as far as us getting into the capsule. Apparently though, when we began to rock to dislodge the board, we sort of redirected the flight path from were we intended to go. We didn't know this till it was too late. Down the hill we went, round and round, laughing the whole way. Suddenly we began hitting small trees. Not enough to stop us but enough to bang us around and get the vehicle rocking from one wheel to the other. It was like being in a car wreck. Finally the thing tipped over on its side, landing with the door down against the ground. It took quite a while for one of us to work a leg free and push upwards enough for the other to crawl out and right the Yodskof.

We had great fun with our new creation and were proud of it. We decided to show it off to our friends at the other end of Bellevue. We wheeled it up the valley road to the highway and along the highway to the upper end of Bellevue. The kids there gathered round to see a demonstration flight. The highway was already a dead end road at that time with only local traffic to worry about. Doug entered the Yodskof at the near end of upper Bellevue. This was at the top of a long and very gentle slope, and we planned to pilot him down the highway to the other end of the neighborhood and then let someone else take a ride. We started him along with all of us walking alongside. It wasn't long before I realized that while this slope was real gentle, it was really long as well. Also it was blacktop highway, and that made for good rolling conditions. *Really* good rolling conditions. Soon we were trotting alongside the spool and then running. I realized that we were flying in conditions we had never experienced before and that just like that early test flight, we were about to lose control of the situation. I tried to slow the Yodskof down but I couldn't and it began to pull away from me. About the time it left me in the dust I heard the "thumpety thump thump" of Doug flopping around inside. Our record speed coupled with the un-cushioned ride over the blacktop had been too much for the human body. Even the body of an adventure hardened veteran country boy like Doug. He was unconscious inside and lost his "bracing" grip. On the bright side, he had no clue as to the danger he was in.

    The Yodskof hurtled down the blacktop followed by a screaming mob. As I look back on it now, the other kids probably thought this was all part of our demonstration. It didn't take long for them to realize though, that Doug was headed for trouble. The crick crossed the road just ahead and he might well end up in it. Or he might just crash into the concrete sideguards. Luckily, just as he neared the crick the capsule careened off the road and came to a relatively gentle stop. Doug regained consciousness and was climbing out just as we ran up.

    The Yodskof flew many more successful flights. I think that was our last on blacktop though. It's memories like this one that make me wonder how any of us survived to adulthood.

11

Young Love, First Love

While I realize that there is no better way to elicit an angry snarl from your Alpha Female than to talk about your past loves; this story is about pivotal moments and memorable happenings of my youth. Thus, I am compelled to relate the circumstances surrounding the first occasion when cupid's arrow found its mark deep within my breast. That so few of the details are clear in my memory gives testament to how long ago this occurred. The fact that I remember what I do gives testament to how much of an impact the incident had on me.

We of my gender are at a definite disadvantage when it comes to romance. The female seems born ready for romance and knows her role. She talks about it freely with her friends and even plays with "bride" dolls. A girl can always tell her girlfriends when she is sweet on some guy, and they all think it's great. Not so for the male of the species. Nearly all of us men have a romantic side and believe it or not it kicks in early for most of us too. However, you don't talk about it until you and your entire circle of male friends have *all* reached the point in your life when you seek and will accept romantic relationships. Naturally, learning where your peers are at with their romantic development is tricky because you just don't talk about those things. This is what cripples us for life in the romance department. Being of Finnish descent, the reserved nature of the Finn makes such talk even more difficult. I suppose the fact that I grew up in a house full of girls might have made me different than a lot of guys. I certainly learned how to walk on eggshells when I was very young. But I heard a lot of open talk of romance too. My older sisters talked about boys and had boyfriends over, and I even saw Carol kiss one of them one time when she was supposed to be babysitting us younger ones. They played records and the radio, and of course all of that music is romantic. Perhaps this has helped me to overcome some of the hurdles we men face. On more than one occasion I have expressed my affection for my Alpha Female of twenty-eight years by telling her she was cuter than a beagle puppy and more fun than a ten point buck. Such shameless expressions of affection do not come easily to most men.

I guess I was pretty young when thoughts of romance forced their way in amongst the thoughts of frog hunting and other important things. Not that I would share these thoughts with anyone, heavens to Betsy no. In fact, I won't share a lot of it now. All I will say is that it wasn't sexual and that it was pure romance. I liked listening to some of those songs and thinking that some day love, beautiful love, would enter my life. I didn't have to wait long.

It was my kindergarten year. That's right, kindergarten. Her name was Peggy. She had blonde hair and she wore those curls, I think they are called rag curls but I'm a guy so what do I know about what they were called? But they were beautiful. I think a lot of girls wore their hair that way but none of them looked as good as Peggy. She wore dresses to school. All the girls wore dresses to school then but not one of them had dresses as pretty as the ones Peggy wore. The songs on the radio began to sound even better.

There is an element of torment in such things for the male. I wondered if I was "weird" because I had sure never felt quite like this before. I sure didn't talk about it with anyone. My pals would have teased the crap out of me. Somehow though, I think the influence of my sisters told me these feelings were natural and acceptable. It's rather funny that I never was quite sure about the normalcy of such feelings until I got to junior high and read Tom Sawyer. Mr. Clemens sure had a knack for writing, and when he describes Tom's feelings for Becky Thatcher, I knew what he was talking about, and I knew that I wasn't alone!

So I was smitten. Miss Peggy, my kindergarten classmate, became the object of my heart's desire. But what was one to do about it?

The Bellevue kids were about the first to arrive at school each day, through some quirk in the bus schedule. My neighbor Johnny and I were the first ones in class every morning. We were still days or months away from becoming the young hellions we turned into, so we would go to our seats and sit with hands folded till class began. Peggy lived near the school I think and walked to class. She was usually one of the first to come in after Johnny and me. I don't remember how long it took me to come up with my plan or how long after I came up with it that I actually put it in motion. It was bold, for Johnny would be there. But Johnny was an exceptionally quiet boy so I decided it was worth the risk.

That morning we sat with folded hands, quiet as mice. Peggy came in, hung up her coat, and went to her seat, which was not far from mine. I said her name and when she looked at me, I gave her the "come here" motion with my finger. She came over and I told her I had to "whisper her something". She leaned down and put her ear towards me. Those blonde curls were right there. I didn't hesitate for a second, and I boldly and happily planted a big kiss on her cheek.

She stood up wide-eyed and surprised! Then she smiled the sweetest smile you ever did see, and she blushed, and she went back to her chair and she kept smiling at me and looking at me, and I smiled and looked back. She liked that I had kissed her. It was glorious! I recall that I told my family at supper that night that I had kissed Peggy. I was proud and happy and I didn't care who might find out about it. That's all I remember about it. I don't remember if anyone teased me. I don't remember if I ever so much as talked to Peggy again in my life because she moved away when we were still in grade school. Maybe my heart was broken and it was too traumatic for my conscious mind to retain. I honestly can't remember. What I do remember was that kiss and the look on her face after I kissed her. That my friends, has always been and will always be . . . enough.

12

Ghosts, Goblins, and the Paranormal

All kids are fascinated and terrified by ghost stories and the like. Everyone remembers sitting around a campfire, lying in a backyard tent, or just in bed, talking with other kids about ghosts and aliens and mass murderers. Being scared is a tricky thing. If it weren't fun to be a little bit scared we would never say, "Let's tell ghost stories!" But then you need to know when to quit. Otherwise you get really scared, and then it's one long night in the backyard tent or the embarrassment of chickening out and running home.

We had plenty of the standard stories. The "Urban Legends". I almost called this chapter "Rural Legends" because we sure weren't urban but I didn't think anyone would get what I meant. At any rate we had the same stories that all kids do. There was even a Lover's Lane on the way to Negaunee, a little gravel side road that detoured off of M35 and circled back to it. I am sure that the ditches along this road were full of prosthetic hooked arms and corpses, and I sure hoped that none of my big sisters ever went parking there with their boyfriends. We also had a lot of legends that I think were purely local.

The Professor told me that spirits occupied Bellevue, or at least that some people thought so. He told me that the old man (now deceased) who lived in that little farmhouse in the valley had once plowed up a skeleton in his field. He also said that one of the men who used to drive the bus on our route refused to drive down into the valley because he knew it was haunted. How much of this was fact and how much of it was trying to scare the crap out of the little neighbor kid, I can't tell you. I believed him though. I had seen our dogs on more than one occasion bark and growl and look at "nothing", all their hair standing on end. One time I think I ran in the house when I saw them do this while staring at the side of the garage. Everyone knows that dogs can detect spirits, right?

One story I heard was about an abandoned car in Palmer. On a certain day of the year, the car's doors would open and close and spirit voices could be heard coming from inside of it. A woman's screaming actually. Everyone in Palmer knew about this and knew the date it would happen, and they all stayed in their houses that day. One day an unsuspecting man acquired this car and got it running. It was reported that every time he rode in it at night he felt the presence of someone else in the car with him. Then one day he decided to give the car a good cleaning, and under the floor mats and seats he discovered dried blood and hair. He cleaned this all up, and from then on the car was just a car, and no spirit entities were heard from again.

The rural legend that caused the most stir in the area was that of the "Lady with the Lamp". As you drove from Bellevue to Negaunee, you passed through a location known as Rolling Mill. If you took the Rolling Mill road, there was a portion of it that passed alongside some wide-open meadows, which I imagine were old farm fields. One summer people began to see strange lights out in these meadows. A story began to circulate that these lights were of the spirit world. It seems that years before, a couple had lived near here, and the wife had made a habit of walking towards town with a lantern to meet her husband when he returned from the afternoon shift at one of the mines. One day he was killed in a mining accident, but his grief stricken wife still continued her late night walks with the lantern in hopes he would one-day return to her. She continued this vigil 'til the end of her days, and now her spirit was carrying the lamp. It was big news around Negaunee and even made the newspaper. Someone said it was even written up in a Milwaukee newspaper. Soon crowds were gathering on the road that ran by the meadows. Many of these observers witnessed the lights, and a few of the brave ones even walked out into the fields towards them. Before they could get too close though, the light would disappear and then reappear in another part of the meadow. This was pretty big stuff. I had heard a lot of stories about ghosts but I actually got to participate in this one a little. One of the older neighborhood kids drove a bunch of us out one night so we could get a look at the lights. There were dozens of people there, and cars were parked up and down the road. Unfortunately the Lady with the Lamp didn't show that night. Perhaps her husband's ghost was working day shift.

Eventually it seemed that the Lady with the Lamp got tired of looking for her husband, because the lights were no longer seen. I can't recall how long the phenomenon went on that summer, but as I said, it was big news around the Negaunee area. Later there were rumors that some high school kids set up the whole thing. Four kids with walky talkies and flashlights had made up the story and began bringing people out to see the ghostly mourner. After lights were seen a couple of times word got out and the thing really took off. Two of the perpetrators were in the meadow with lights, and the others would watch the crowd. If anyone got bold enough to walk out towards the light, it was extinguished, and the other "ghost" in another part of the meadow got the word via two way radio to turn on his light.

Often the truth takes a lot of fun out of something. I like the story of the Lady with the Lamp a lot more than the story of four teenagers pulling off a successful hoax. I can't say for sure if there really was a hoax or not. I bet my sister Cheryl can tell you though.

The last of these stories that I will share is pretty spooky. At least for me it is. It is the strange tale of the "Blue Lights".

It was summertime and I was away from Bellevue for a while. I think I had probably been staying with one of my sisters in the big city. When I returned, Bellevue was abuzz with a very strange story.

While I was away an unusual heat wave had taken place. The U.P. is a place where you might have frost on any given day throughout the entire summer. Excessive heat is almost never a problem, but that summer it was. Everyone had trouble sleeping due to the hot and humid weather. Because of the heat, the Professor had been unable to sleep in his room and he had gone out to his car to sleep in hopes that it would be cooler there. During the night he had his close encounter. (I may be getting a few of the details not quite right here but this is what my memory tells me.)

That night he was awakened by something. A strange bluish glow was in the air. He sat up and just outside was a glowing blue orb, hovering outside the car. He shined the flashlight on it and watched it for a while, then bolted for the house. I can't recall now if he woke everyone up to look or what happened but everyone in the neighborhood had heard about the event. I remember people talking about this and wondering what it could have been. It seemed like nobody doubted that it had happened. I think swamp gas was mentioned as a possibility.

Some time later, maybe the same year maybe a year or two later; the Professor was walking home from Negaunee late at night. As he passed an abandoned farm about a mile from his home, there in the woods was another one of these blue lights. I imagine he broke some sort of record covering that last mile home. This was pretty significant because the phenomenon had repeated. After that, a lot of us began hunting for the blue lights.

I made several trips with the Professor and others to that abandoned farm. I was told that several people saw the lights there after those first two sightings but I never did. One night Rod and Doug and I were there with the Professor, and somehow he talked us into leaving the car and walking up an old road above the farm that led to an apple orchard. Doug and I were pretty young, and I remember us telling the older two "You better not try to scare us!" and they promised not to.

We hoofed it around that hill for a while and then decided to get back to the car. Rod was in the lead, barely visible in the darkness as we walked back down the orchard road. Doug and I were side by side, and the Professor was behind us. He just couldn't pass on such a golden opportunity to take a few years off of the neighbor kid's lives I guess, because he let out a shriek that would wake the dead. It just about killed three youngsters too, Doug and I from fright and Rod came near to getting run down as Doug and I took off like rockets into the night. We passed on either side of Rod at something close to light speed. The Professor got a good laugh.

We made a lot of late night trips to that old farm to look for the lights. It seemed like we had a lot of trouble starting the car when we were ready to leave, which added much to the feeling that we were dealing with "ghostly" things. I suppose we would get excited and hit the gas too hard and flood the engine or something. One time we ended up walking home in the dead of night and another time someone came to look for us and rescued us with a jumpstart. I never did get to see one of the blue lights back then, but have seen them often since. But only at Kmart.

13

The Camp

In about 1948, my Dad bought a little piece of ground adjacent to the homestead that my granddad, (Dad's father in law) had carved out of the wilds of Black River Township. It was to be the site of his deer camp, and he and his brothers erected a decent size shack of rough sawn lumber, log rafters, and green and red tarpaper siding. Insulation was in the form of cardboard boxes flattened and nailed to the interior side of the studs. At about the same time just up the hill a stone's throw away, a house was also built for my grandparents, Mummu and Faari Ruuska. Mummu and Faari are the terms we used for grandma and grandpa. Uncle George Ruuska lived on the original homestead. There was a bumpy black topped road that snaked its way between the homestead and the new structures. One direction would take you to the little town of Republic, the other back towards Negaunee and home. It was country that had been farmed, but by the time I saw it the farming was done. It was typical rocky and rugged Upper Peninsula terrain, and the local residents had combined farming in the summer and woodcutting in the winter. These activities tend to make great deer cover and thus great deer hunting country. The camp was a refuge for Dad and great fun for me.

Of the ten homes closest to the camp, six belonged to Aunts and Uncles. It was cousin rich country. Our summer stays there with the whole family were about as close as I came to a trip to Disney World when I was a tyke. Shooting the 22 and fishing with Dad, visiting the relatives and getting into mischief with the cousins. Sometimes we would swim at "the bend" on the river or at Perna's Lake. (The Perna family were cousins of course). "Mummu and Faari" just up the hill, were pretty old already, and spoke little English but they were a pleasant pair of grandparents as far as I was concerned. Charley, my bachelor uncle, lived with them, and he would help me build chipmunk traps and we would set them by the sauna in the piney woods. One year we caught two at one time and the first day they managed to escape from the holding cage inside the camp. We had some real wild chases trying to recapture them, not succeeding for several days. When we would wake up in the morning, often the fugitive chippies were sitting on the blankets at our feet nibbling away at breadcrumbs and other food they had found. My cousin Lenny and I once cut down one of those pine trees near the sauna. We got in a little bit of trouble for this, because it was simply wasteful. Thirty years or so later Lenny (who had acquired the land) cut the whole stand of pines down and sold the wood. I teased him a bit about this, but in his defense, he replanted the entire area with pine.

Usually in the evening we would visit at the home of one of the relatives. A sauna bath was often part of the program. With the long summer days, we often timed our return to the camp for dusk. Then the drill was to cover the food and dishes, fill the place with "bug bomb" to take care of the mosquitoes that had penetrated the defenses during the day and take a spin around cousins instead of with the family. Trout fishing, grouse hunting, or just having fun with the guys, the camp was a headquarters for all of that. When I was about 13 we moved into Negaunee, and after the first year of really having fun being a town kid, I was wishing I were back in Bellevue. If I couldn't live in the country, I decided I would spend as much time there as I could. With the camp as a base of operations where I could spend the night without getting in anyone's way, Black River became my second home. In those simpler times, hitchhiking was a pretty well accepted mode of travel for kids my age, and I thumbed many a ride to the camp. The first twenty miles were easy, the last several could be tough because of the lack of traffic on those roads. If a car did come by though, the driver was either related to me or knew me and usually picked me up. I remember once when cousin Johnny was over, we decided we should hitch hike to the camp for the weekend, but we wanted to take guns. We were able to take apart the old 22 as it was built to break in two with a thumbscrew and a 12 gauge single shot also broke down to small pieces except for the barrel. We got everything into our gym bags or whatever we had, except that barrel. John wrapped his coat around it and made like he was carrying the coat by the collar, letting it hang free. If he watched how he moved you couldn't tell there was anything inside.

We got a ride right off the bat, and I jumped in the front seat, John in the back. We struck up some friendly chatter with the driver and were cruising down US41 when I glanced back at John. He was blabbing away and looking out the window, and his coat was standing straight up on the back seat of the car, his hand just holding on to the bottom of it and resting on the seat! The driver either didn't notice it or maybe thought our moms starched the laundry pretty heavily.

Through 1972, the camp was a headquarters for my pals and me, besides being the deer-hunting shack. It still stands there and houses a mess of Prusi's each November. My cousins, Rod and Chas, bought it from Mom, improved it and maintain it. It

Black River looking for deer. After allowing time for the spray to clear and the mosquitoes to expire we returned and hit the sack. Those of us who were "mature" enough got to be on the top bunk, and the frogs and a whippoorwill sang our lullaby.

In the morning it was time for another day of adventure. Often it started with a brief battle over who got what box of cereal from the "snack pack" we always had, the camp trips being the only time we ever saw these little cereal boxes. We picked wild strawberries on the hill next to the camp and put them in a bowl with milk and sugar. We turned the bunk beds into stagecoaches by hanging blankets around them. The two sets of bunks were side by side, so you could (with the good imagination of a kid) race each other, but it always ended in a tie. We could leap back and forth on the coach tops and tussle with the other crew. Between my three younger sisters and I, and the constant parade of cousins, there were not a lot of empty seats in our coaches.

Cousin Lenny's house was a lot of fun, it being the homestead of my grandparents. There was the old barn foundation with the cattle stanchions still in place to climb around on. An old sawmill in the woods, run by Uncle Bill Ruuska at some time, had all kinds of old equipment and buildings and a big sawdust pile. We had a great imaginary cannon that was a wheeled axle with a long pipe of a tongue that we propped up with a stick (or something) to get the elevation we needed to launch our deadly imaginary shells deep into The Third Reich. There were sandbanks that had this kind of chunky, clumpy, very fine sand. We would toss the chunks into the air and when they hit they exploded like artillery shells. It was great fun. Uncle George logged, and Lenny had to help, but when we were around he got a little extra time off. We would scramble around the "pulp woods" or the "balsam bush" having pine cone fights and climbing trees.

As time went on, and interests changed, the camp consistently remained a place for having a great time. As soon as I was old enough to be trusted (actually I wasn't to be trusted yet but the folks didn't know) I began going to the camp with friends and holds a special place in their hearts too, for they hunted there during the deer seasons of their youth and also vacationed at the camp in the summer. I hope, I dearly hope, that their sons who now hunt there will form the same attachment for the place as the first two generations of owners did. I hope that "Walt's Camp" remains an institution for *at least* another fifty years.

14

Christmas

It started with the catalogs. Sears, J.C. Penney, and Montgomery Ward. Big, thick catalogs for the Christmas season. Sometime in the fall they arrived, and every kid in the house was anxious to get a look at what new toys were available this Christmas. The Wish Books. We combed the pages of the toy sections. The normal catalogs didn't have toy sections but the Christmas Wish Books did. We looked at all of it and then started the process of deciding what we wanted most. When I had my selections pretty well settled, I would share them with Rod and Doug, and they would show me their own choices. Commercialism and greed at Christmas time have been around for a long time I guess. We learned about it pretty early in our lives even in Bellevue.

There is so much going on for kids at Christmas time. I remember going on shopping trips with the folks to Ishpeming. Snowy sidewalks and Christmas carols playing and crowded stores. Just like the song says. The scene of the streetlights and music and decorations and falling snow are common to most of us and also special to most of us because people really are just a little bit nicer at Christmas time.

 Dad would get us a tree. No bought trees for the thrifty Prusi clan when all it took was a hike in the woods with your axe to get one. I tagged along with Dad sometimes, and if I didn't go along when he got the tree from the woods, I was sure to be at his heels when he mounted it in the old red and green metal stand and set it up. I remember that Auntie Jennie was particular about her Christmas tree. When Rod and Doug were given the tree assignment it took them a little while to learn what their mom expected I guess, because one year there were several rejects outside their house in the snow bank before one finally made the grade. We didn't do a whole lot of decorating other than the tree itself, but there were a few decorations around the house. My favorite was a small village of paper or cardboard houses and stores with tiny lights inside each one.

 There was a series of events to participate in at Christmas time. We drew names, both at home and at school and I think even at Sunday school. You hoped you got the name of one of your pals because it was so much more fun to go gift shopping for a guy than for some girl. Then of course you had the party at school and the one at Sunday school. I remember that one of the popular gifts at the school parties was a book of Lifesaver candy. It opened like a book and was filled with rolls of the little candies in every flavor you could think of and some you couldn't. It seems like every year several kids in my class got one of these, and I really wanted one. Finally I got one when I was in about fourth grade. Never have I eaten myself so sick of candy as I did that year, and I hoped I would never see another one of those books. There was also a party at the Prusi farm where Dad grew up, for all the uncles and aunts and cousins. The last time I attended one of these was in the 1970's after I was married. What I remember about the Prusi party was that Santa Claus usually showed up. He was a pretty lame Santa. I'm not sure who got the job of playing the jolly elf, I suppose it was one of the uncles. If so, they were much better uncles than they were Santa. In spite of the fact that Santa called me an "ole' stick in the mud" one time, Christmas was Christmas and the party was fun.

Where I first attended school, the Kirkpatrick School in Palmer, the Christmas plays were a big event. In the school we had grades one through six, and each class participated. This was an exciting event. It was held during the evening, and at least a couple of times the school bus picked us up just as they would for a school day. It was exciting to ride the bus at night. One time my Mom even rode the bus with me to the play. Parents were allowed to ride on the bus for the Christmas play. Being at the school at night was different and exciting. We usually went to our classroom and waited there till it was our turn to perform. After our performance we returned to the classroom, and our family would pick us up there. I remember when I was in Kindergarten or first grade, when Mom came to get me, my sisters Susie and Kathy were with her. When they came in the room my little sisters saw me sitting at my desk. They walked down the aisles to me, one on either side and tried to sit alongside me on my chair. Somehow they both got on that chair and sat there quiet as mice. I really felt like a big brother.

In addition to the usual singing, we sometimes put on little skits at the Kirkpatrick School Christmas Program. One year we got to play instruments. I think they were called Symphonettes or something like that. Long before the play, each kid in my class was issued one of these little plastic flutes. It came in a clear plastic bag, and it had a little metal piece that clipped onto the top of it where you could put your miniature sheet of music. We practiced them during our music class and were also supposed to practice our tunes at home. I wasn't real gifted in the musical department, and though I tried at first to learn to play, I soon gave up. I was a little concerned that my sour notes would stand out at the play. But when the time came for us to show our stuff, it was pretty much just a bunch of unrecognizable tooting.

There was a classmate of mine named Jeffrey who was very small for his age and who could sing beautifully. He got to sing solos on occasion and how I envied him! It wasn't so much that I wanted to be able to sing well, but I wished I had the courage to get up in front of the crowd the way he did. I would have given almost anything to have his self-confidence. This was especially true the time when he got to take part in one of the skits. He played a little boy and a sixth grade girl named Betty played his mom. Betty was . . . mature. We boys all liked to look at Betty. I remember being green with envy when we watched the dress rehearsal, and Jeffrey got to be up there on stage next to Betty!

The big event for us though, was the party with the cousins next door. One year we would host and the next year they would. It was always on Christmas Eve so I suppose that added to the excitement of this particular party. The excitement of the season is at fever pitch on Christmas Eve. We had "drawn names" earlier, and now we got to get our "name gift". Doug and I often knew what we were gonna get because each of us knew where the family gift stash was, and we would sometimes give each other a preview of the gift we'd be getting on Christmas Eve. Besides the gift business, it was fun to have us all together. Mom and Auntie Jennie had done their Christmas baking with the help of the "big girls" and there were lots of treats. Prune tarts and candy cane cookies were two that I remember, and there were real candy canes and other hard candy around for the only time during the year. There was also "pop" in great abundance, and that didn't happen in our house except at Christmas. It was from Elson's Bottling Works. Dad would get a whole wooden crate of the big glass bottles. Strawberry, orange, ginger ale, cream soda, and other flavors. It was swell.

After the party we all adjourned to our respective homes, and for the kids there was that long sleepless night. Then the joy of the morning gift orgy. Like so many kids I remember sneaking down in the wee hours and having my breath taken away by a living room full of gifts. The picture I have in my mind is not of any particular toy or toys but rather that of the tree in the dim light and the glittering decorations and gifts everywhere.

I had once asked my folks what Christmas was like for them as far as gifts went, and it made me sad to learn that sometimes there was only a small token gift for each kid in their family. One time Dad got some colored paper to draw on. I never remember a Christmas that we didn't get a lot of gifts. There had to have been some rough times because of strikes, layoffs, or when Dad was laid up with a broken shoulder hurt in an accident at the mine. Still, it seems like they always found a way to get us plenty of gifts. Christmas miracle perhaps?

As we got older and the "big kids" began to move away from home to begin their own lives, one of the nice things about Christmas was having them come home to visit. Some were married and eventually nieces and nephews became part of the program, and we would anxiously await the late night arrivals of our big sisters and their husbands and their kids. I remember Rod and Doug and me being so excited about our nieces and nephews. Of course, my folks and Bill and Jenny were just like grandparents ought to be. I remember Dad getting some basic woodworking power tools and building wooden rocking horses for Kevin and Robbie, his two oldest grandsons. These were given as Christmas gifts. It was after our big sisters got married that we spent our first Christmas away from Bellevue as a couple of times we traveled to be with them at their homes for the holidays.

Rod and Doug and I got a lot of gifts that were cowboy or soldier related things. I had hundreds of the little plastic toy figures. World War II soldiers, Civil War soldiers, Indians and what have you. Doug had many as well. We all had lots of toy guns and played army and cowboys all the time. We watched war movies late at night. When we were small we thought soldiers were cool, which they are, and we thought war was pretty cool, which is wrong but we were just kids. I know that these days toy guns are sort of frowned upon by a lot of people and I don't see as many of the toy soldiers in the stores as we did back then. I guess people think that playing with such things might be a recipe for turning out bad kids. But in our day, we shot up the neighborhood all the time in our play, and none of us turned into criminals in our adult lives.

But I was talking about soldiers.

In 1962 we got our own soldier in the family. Chas joined the army and left home for three years. He is ten years older than I and was one of my heroes just as he was to his younger brothers Rod and Doug. When he became a soldier we were in awe. I remember when he got promoted to sergeant Rod and Doug couldn't wait to tell me. I also remember my Mom saying how that song "Mr. Lonely" made her want to cry because she thought of Chas so far away from all of us.

At Christmas time in 1964, a young soldier was spotted walking down the road from the highway. Our soldier boy had gotten leave and surprised everyone when he showed up at home. I can't recall who spotted him or those exact details but the good news got to our house very quickly. It seems like we just boiled out of the house when we heard Chas was home and ran to Bill and Jennie's. There he was sitting at the table in the little breakfast nook in their kitchen. There were people sitting all around the table and standing in the kitchen. Everyone was talking and everyone was happy. More than happy. Joyful is a better word. Chas was beaming. I can't tell you who all was in the kitchen right then. I mean it's pretty easy to guess but I don't recall anyone in particular except for Chas, and I can still see him with his army haircut and that huge happy smile. I felt so happy and excited and was a little puzzled because I felt tears in my eyes. I guess that I had never cried with happiness before.

At the beginning of this chapter I wrote that we learned about greed and the commercialism of Christmas early in life, but we learned other important things early in life as well. I don't remember what I got for gifts that year, or the party, or much of anything else particularly well. But I will never forget the joy that filled that kitchen when our soldier came home for Christmas.

15

Forting Up

We did a lot of cowboy and Indian stuff in the valley. We were Lewis and Clark, Daniel Boone, Mosby's Raiders, Marines, and Indian warriors. Many a daring expedition was mounted to conquer our enemies or the wilderness. I read so many books about such people and would emulate them in my play. I remember reading about John Colter and how he was the first white man to discover Yellowstone, and I was fascinated by the accounts of his adventures there. I had seen Yellowstone on television, and Bill and Jennie went there with their younger kids once, bringing home pictures and a first hand account. What was more fascinating to me was the idea of wandering into such a place when nobody had seen such things before and with no people around save the wild savages and the land teeming with game. I spent a lot of time that spring pretending I was John Colter exploring "Colter's Hell", as Yellowstone was called back then.

We made pretend horses and saddles by hanging old tires on

the fence posts and sitting on top of them, pretending we were tall in the saddle. I read one book about a young Sioux Indian growing up and how he learned to hunt and train his horse for hunting buffalo. Then I would stand up several tires in the yard alongside my fence-post-and-tire horse and mount up with my bow and arrows, shooting the other tires and knocking them down. We dragged our "supplies" out in the fields and up onto the hill and made "camps". We once had a civil war encampment in the yard complete with barrels and stacked muskets. But even rugged Plains Indians and Lewis and Clark needed more permanent places to rest and recover and we were no different. We learned to build "forts".

I will sort of lump tents and tepees and camps and forts all together here. We had them all. You start out your fort building when you're pretty small. Throwing blankets over the kitchen table is a good beginner fort, as are large cardboard boxes. You outgrow these pretty quickly though and move on to bigger and better things outdoors. One of our first outdoor camps was made from a steel tube hammock frame. We turned it upside down and threw old rugs over it. This was where Doug and I made our first backyard camping attempt. I ended up chickening out and going inside. Much to my surprise, Doug stuck it out *all by himself!* In the morning I got up and ran out to look into the tent, and there he was, sleeping like a babe! He was such a brave kid! I succeeded in my second attempt.

We took over a couple of abandoned cars for camps over the years. One was an old Model T or Model A. It was just the body of the old wreck but some of the old levers and dials were still in it. We played in it like it was our car for years, and eventually Doug and I turned it into a camp that was nicely appointed with candles and wooden crates for furniture. We were into pipe smoking then, and we hid our pipes and tobacco there. Unfortunately while I was away on a trip Doug somehow managed to burn it down. Thank goodness I had my pipe hidden elsewhere.

Occasionally we got to take over actual buildings. When the house at the end of the road was vacated, we appropriated a small outbuilding for a while as our headquarters. Then for one or two summers my Dad let us take over the garage. This was a great facility, the only problem with it being was that it was too nice, and the girls wanted to use it too so we had to share custody.

During our savage Indian phase, (no I am not talking about my entire childhood) Doug and I built an Indian village. It was in the woods near the base of the big bluff. We cut poles and leaned them against a larger tree, going completely around it in a circle just like real teepee poles. We then cut pine and balsam boughs and laid them over the poles. Now I know that real Indians used buffalo hide but we had not seen many buffalo around that year so made do with what we had. We made two of these teepees just a few yards apart. We had bows and arrows and spears and knives hung here and there around the village, handy in case our enemies showed up or the buffalo finally came around. We made a fire ring out of rocks and put together war paint kits. These were simply different colored rocks. You could spit on a rock and then grind another rock against it, and the dust and the spit together made great war paint. It was hard to get much of a color selection but again we did the best with what we had. I can remember what that stuff felt like when it dried on my cheeks! We even had ourselves a totem pole, hand carved and planted into a hole we dug for it. The village was a great place, and I think Doug and I sort of kept it to ourselves. Then one day after we had been playing there and had a fire in our fire ring, a fire truck showed up on our street. The driver said an airplane pilot had reported a smoldering haystack back in the woods. We had to abandon the village for a while till things cooled off.

Snow forts were common and because they are so temporary they don't stand out in my mind, except for a huge one we had one winter. It was at the end of the street near Uncle Bill's garage. The plows had made a huge bank there, and the snow was packed nice and firm. We worked on it for days. I think it had to have been seventy-five feet long. It ran right alongside the road, and we dug trenches and piled up the snow we dug to form protective walls. There were several nice rooms connected by the trench that ran the length of the fort. At one end we had sort of a tower.

Inside these battlements we stockpiled snowballs. We also had spears that were made from the wooden lathe that was used for snow fencing. There were plenty of spears and snowballs. But the most unique feature of this fort was our escape tunnel. We had sleds of course and used them a lot. We decided we needed a quick way to mount our sleds and escape in case the enemy was about to overwhelm us. So we dug a tunnel from the surface of the road, through the bank, and up into the fort. We covered the tunnel entrance with a piece of plywood and packed snow over that. With our sleds inside the fort, we could duck behind the walls, jump on the sled, and burst through the secret door and onto the icy street and be away in a flash. Sort of. The wooden door sometimes got hung up under your sleigh runners, and the road was fairly flat there so we couldn't get up much speed. But what an idea!

The be all and end all of our forts though, our masterpiece, was the tree fort. It still makes me proud when I think of it.

The adventure started out with us hauling lumber, from who knows where to the top of the hill. Initially Doug and I each made a fort in trees that stood about thirty yards apart. Mine had a nice window overlooking the valley and mounted in the center of this window was a huge slingshot that I had made. I had visions of being able to launch shotgun like handfuls of iron ore pellets far down into the valley but the design was flawed, and it didn't shoot well at all. We had the two forts connected with the old tin can and string telephone system for a while. Then we decided we should pool our resources into one grand fort, and we tore down my structure and used the lumber to add on to Doug's, and I became a full partner in its ownership. We had some help from Rod and the Professor I know, but it still had to have been quite a project. The results were, in a word, spectacular. Let me give you the tour.

To get to our Mother of All Forts you walked up the hill behind Bill and Jennie's. As you passed Slide Rock, the flat sloping rock that we used as a playground and where we carved our names with hammers and railroad spikes, you would bear a little to your right. At the top of the hill you would walk past the

"Burpy" tree where we played a made up game of chase or tag using my toy burp gun. Past this you looked to your left and there it was. There was a nice path with large rocks placed on either side, and all along its course. The path divided, one branch going to the fort, and the other to a little spring that bubbled out of the rocks for most of the year. There was at least one cow skull mounted on a pole stuck in the ground alongside the path and several ominous "Danger—No Trespassing" signs that had found their way from the Empire Mine perimeter fence to our fort.

The fort itself was in a cedar tree. To gain entrance you climbed the limbs, and as you climbed you sort of circled from the back side to the front, eventually coming to a ladder that we had fixed to the front of the fort and along one edge. The ladder took you to an opening in the middle story of the fort. You climbed in through this window and you were in the fort now. The room was about four-foot square, and this room was all enclosed except for that entrance. There was a bench, some shelves, and no doubt plenty of slingshot ammo in coffee cans. In the floor was a trapdoor that gave you access to the lowest floor. This level had windows on, I think, three sides, and they were screened in with chicken wire. There was a tin box mounted to the wall like a medicine cabinet for storage. To get to the top floor you needed to get back to the ladder outside and go up. The third floor was open except for a low railing around the entire level. This "deck" was covered with a roof, and if you were nimble, you could actually get up to the top of the roof by climbing tree limbs. It was awesome.

I know that we had a lot of other interesting things inside the fort and around the grounds but I can't recall all of them. But it was a nice retreat for country boys. From its confines we could watch what was going on down in the valley and also be close to the bluff and the woods. It was sort of an outpost of our civilization. It only got us in trouble one time that I remember, and that was when the girls tried to crash the place. We had to resort to our slingshots to drive them off. Cousin Chrissy took one in the noggin, and we got in trouble. That was the only unfortunate incident that I recall in the history of our three-story tree fort.

16

The Mines

My first job after high school was working in the same underground iron mine that my father had worked in till the very day he died. It was called the Mather B mine, and I believe that it was the last operating underground iron ore mine in the country. It too is closed now. Working there was an interesting experience. I got to see the dark musty tunnels that my Dad had to work in for over thirty years and where twice he almost died. I met many of the men he had talked about. Each miner had his last name and first initial on his helmet so if I saw someone with a name and initial that Dad had mentioned I would ask them "Are you BILL Smith?" for example. They would look at my helmet and ask if I was Walt's boy. They all had kind words to say about my Dad, and I remember their generosity and compassion when he passed away. Several of them also told me that he had always hoped I wouldn't go to work in the mine.

One of the jobs I had while at the Mather B was "pocket

man". Pocket men ran the loading chute doors that filled the train cars with the ore. When my boss brought me out to the pocket for the first time and introduced me to the man who would train me, I was pleasantly surprised because the man was my former neighbor Denny, who grew up right across the street from me in Bellevue! The pocket man actually had control of the string of ore cars in that the track was on a gradual slope, and the pocket man controlled the pneumatic brakes that held it there. When a car was full you opened the brakes and let the train begin to coast downhill, and then you stopped it when the next empty car was in place. Once you had a train fully loaded, you called for a locomotive, and it coupled itself to your string of cars and pulled away to another plant where the raw ore was pelletized. The train tracks from the Mather B ran right past our church, and the rumble and roar of a passing ore train drowned out many a sermon. A couple of times I was working while I knew that church services were going on, and when my train pulled out I found it sort of funny thinking about my friends and family about to be interrupted by the fruits of my labor!

I only worked at "The B" for a few weeks, and then a group of us newer fellows was transferred to the Empire Mine. This is the mine near Bellevue, the one that would eventually swallow up our little valley and cause us to leave. It was a surface mine and I worked there for about six months. From the top of some of the buildings I could almost see Bellevue, and it struck me as rather odd that I was working there. As a kid, you see, I spent a lot of time trying to sneak into this very mine. At the Empire I ran into a former neighbor that I hadn't seen in years. He had grown up on that dairy farm in the "upper" part of Bellevue. Again it was the name on the helmet. I recognized the last name and with the first initial "A", I asked if he was Alvin. As usual he looked at my helmet and smiled and said, "Are you Danny?" So we had a mini Bellevue reunion there in the ball mill that we were repairing.

The company that I worked for, for almost thirty years, builds radiators and other cooling system components for heavy equipment including mining vehicles. When I worked on the shop floor I was an inspector for several years and looked at nearly every crate that we shipped out. Many were bound for the mines in Upper Michigan including the Empire. I made a habit out of writing a message inside these crates and signing my name. More than once I got back reports of people I knew seeing these messages when the parts arrived.

Obviously mining and the mines in and around Negaunee and Palmer have played quite a role in my life for my work has revolved around them. Naturally mines are not supposed to be a playground for kids, and the mining companies go to great lengths to keep kids away from the danger there. But for my cohorts and me, fences and no trespassing signs just made a place that much more appealing.

When mining began in Marquette County in the late 1800's, laws to protect the environment were nonexistent and probably not even dreamed of. Negaunee and the surrounding area showed the scars. Old surface mines were reddish brown scars on the landscape; some of them, now filled with water, formed manmade lakes. The underground mines in some cases began to cave in and create sinkholes. Iron Street, the main street in downtown Negaunee has gotten a lot shorter in my lifetime as more and more ground either caved in or threatened to, and the people moved and the area was fenced off. Abandoned buildings and scrap-iron could be found here, there, and everywhere. A lot of these areas were fenced off and posted with warning signs but a lot of them were not. The ones without fences were of little or no interest to us. Those with fences and signs were like bait, and the active mines that had fence, signs, and "mine cops" were like challenges.

The Mary Charlotte mine was between Bellevue and Negaunee. Long since abandoned, a few buildings stood not far from the highway. We took to rummaging through them. We found boxes and boxes of old cancelled paychecks. They were scattered about, and the roof of the building was going, so many were becoming soggy and spoiled but many were in good condition. We pretended we were taking home real paychecks. We found odds and ends and curiosities here but nothing real significant. The fence around the Mary Charlotte buildings was not maintained so it was no challenge.

After leaving Bellevue, my pals and I discovered a huge sinkhole just outside Negaunee in a caving ground area that was fenced off. It was a giant, cone shaped hole in the ground with water in the bottom of it. It was a great swimming hole as the edges were sandy like a beach. You could dive right from shore, the sides so steep you were in six feet of water just a few feet from shore. We began to swim here regularly one summer till those dreaded mine cops got wind of us doing so and ran us out of there one day. I was fleet of foot now, so they didn't catch me. We heard later that when some of the guys went back to check if the coast was clear, the water had all drained out of the sinkhole. I suppose it found its way into a lower level of an old mine or maybe it was pumped out. At any rate, I often thought how exciting it would have been to be swimming there when someone pulled that plug and to perish in the biggest "swirly" in human history. (I digress.)

The Empire Mine was a newer operation. It was just a few miles from our house, and it seems that I can remember talk of the new mine coming. It all seemed to be positive talk. New mines meant jobs, and there are never enough of those to go around in the central Upper Peninsula. I think there was even talk that we wouldn't be in Bellevue much longer but I didn't pay much attention. What I do remember clearly is that we now could hear the heavy equipment running twenty-four hours a day. In the summer when the windows were open the distant roar of the huge trucks and dozers sort of put me to sleep. Blasts from the mine shook our windows. But the most dramatic change that I remember, the one that seemed to have the most impact on me, was the change to the railroad tracks. Not to the tracks themselves, but to the "salvage" that now abounded along the tracks. The Empire Mine turned the ore into pellets right on site, and they were transported down "our" railroad tracks on their way to the docks in Marquette, where they were then loaded on ships. Each day dozens, maybe hundreds of ore cars traveled down the tracks loaded with the pellets, sometimes still steaming from the drying process. Sometimes the cars were a bit overloaded I guess, or maybe the pocket men at Empire were not as good as I would later become at the Mather B. They spilled a lot of pellets along the side rails and other parts of the ore cars as they loaded them. These pellets shook off of the cars as they rode along the tracks, and soon the railroad bed was buried with pellets. They were a half foot deep in places I am sure, all along the tracks. So what use did a country boy have for iron ore pellets? Let me tell you brother, if you don't know you ain't never carried a slingshot. The pellets, while not perfectly round, are spherical. Spherical objects fly much more accurately from a slingshot than plain, old, picked up from the ground, rocks. We were awash in slingshot ammo, and we made the most of it. I don't know how many trips we made hauling three pound coffee cans full of pellets from the tracks to our various hideaways and forts. I don't know how many pounds of pellets fit where three pounds of coffee does but they were a load to carry.

Beyond this windfall of ammo, the Empire provided great recreational opportunities. First I should describe the layout a little. As you left the valley in Bellevue and went towards Palmer, the railroad tracks were parallel to the highway. When you got to the other part of Bellevue the tracks were very close to the road. Along this whole part of the trip, it was pretty much open field astride the road and tracks but as you left the last house behind, the forest came close to the road, and the tracks were screened from view. It was near here that you first saw the fence that surrounded the mine, complete with those ominous "Danger— No Trespassing" signs. The fence was in view pretty much the entire drive to Palmer. You had to drive past "downtown" Palmer to get to the mine entrance, and it was at this far end that the processing plant was located. Between the plant facility and Bellevue was a sort of moonscape where the land had been stripped of trees in preparation for eventual mining.

    I suppose I should tell you a little bit about "mine cops". The "word" was that the mine cops always drove around in yellow pickup trucks looking to spoil the fun of adventurous boys. At school we heard lots of mine cop stories and tales of incredible escapes and occasional captures. Much exaggerated to be sure but the stories sounded just sooooo good, there was no reason to clutter them up with the truth. As I learned later, all the mine vehicles not used for earth moving were yellow pickup trucks. Foremen drove them here and there doing their jobs, and I even got to drive one later when I worked at the Empire. There *were* real security people around the mine properties on occasion. These guys even wore uniforms. Since the mining industry has gone downhill, I think they have all gone to work at shopping malls around the country. These are small points. To us an adult in the mine with a hard hat, who took an interest in spoiling our fun, was a mine cop.

    I am not sure how long the mine was in operation before I first tested its perimeter defenses. I am pretty darn sure I wasn't the first kid in the neighborhood to do so. It wasn't much of a challenge. The fence was no barrier to country boys; our main concern about it was that it would slow us down quite a lot if we had to make a quick escape. Actually the first "penetration" I made was accomplished by walking down the railroad tracks right into the mine. There was no gate; the fence just had a gap in it for the tracks to run through. The "big break" of getting into the mine was pretty anticlimactic.

    We liked to roam that moonscape and look for things. We didn't find much except blasting wire and survey stakes. The wire was "used" and lay helter-skelter all over the area, and it turned out to be handy for a hundred things. We hoarded miles of it. Where I grew up, because of the mining industry there was a pretty intense public service warning program in place to warn people about blasting caps. These are the small explosive devices used to detonate larger charges. They are sort of harmless looking but can be awfully dangerous. There were ads on television and posters in the schools showing you what they looked like and what they could do. We were very lucky that none of those wire trails we followed ended at a blasting cap or a live unexploded charge.

Perhaps most interesting were the mine-related things we encountered. The railroad bed was upgraded at one point, and there were bundles of ties and kegs of spikes and metal plates. We had fun watching the workers but more fun when they left. Old spikes were handy for all kinds of things but I can't remember what any of them were. The wooden kegs were pretty cool too, and we helped ourselves to a lot of these discarded articles. I can almost smell them as I am writing this. The tracks crossed the highway at one point and there were the old fashioned railroad crossing signs. They were in the shape of an X and across one leg of the X it said RAILROAD and across the other, CROSSING. Little reflectors that resembled miniature light bulbs formed these letters. One time they replaced the signs and left the old ones laying there, so we got ourselves a supply of the reflectors. Along the tracks were burned out railroad flares, and we picked up their remains as curiosities. These things seem so insignificant as I write them down but they were such interesting articles to us kids. We put nails and coins and what have you on the rails and collected them later, flattened thin by the train wheels. Always, we were a little worried we would derail a train. Near the crossing there was a wooden box mounted on a post with a phone in it. I suppose it ran to the mine or who knows where. On the wooden box was stenciled X3R. It was padlocked all the time. Except for once. We found the box open and picked up the phone. There was no dial, only a button. So we pushed the button and started talking. "X3R X3R come on in." We said in a voice as official and grown up sounding as we could. The response crackled out of the box. "YOU G__ D___ KIDS GET OFF THAT PHONE AND GET THE H__ OUT OF THERE!"

We complied with the dispatcher request.

The trains themselves were occasionally "hopped" for a ride. They had convenient ladders on the sides of them which I like to think were put there just for us. We also ran alongside the moving trains and plucked out little cardboard tags that had been placed on each car. Why? Good question. Because they were there maybe. Later when I grew up and became a "pocket man" I had to fill these cards out and put them on the cars. It struck me as very funny.

There was a gravel pit alongside the tracks right near where the valley road intersected with the highway. On many occasions this area was used as sort of a supply depot or off loading spot. During the construction of a pipeline of some kind, the area was filled with old tires that were used as cushions between the ground, and the pipe that was being unloaded from rail cars. The tires were left behind. Some of them were huge tires from the giant haul trucks that operated inside the mine and neighborhood kids piled them up and made a tunnel with a tower at each end. For the same pipeline project a boxcar load of Styrofoam insulation was brought in. It came in sheets and it was light blue. It carved easily and floated nicely, and you could carry a lot of it away at a time. There were a lot of blue Styrofoam boats and cars and what have you around the neighborhood for quite a while. One day around this time the folks were driving home from Negaunee when down the hill from the tracks came a rather large tire, bouncing and moving along at a good clip, crossing the highway and continuing down into the valley. Again the mine and railroad folks had provided recreational opportunities for the local ragamuffins. I believe there was some fallout from the "tires cross the highway" incident and can happily report that I was not involved. I am not sure who was involved but I bet Rod knows.

I was talking about the mine. We made a lot of forays into the Empire, and once or twice saw those dreaded yellow trucks and imagined that they were headed our way. Always we took flight and later congratulated ourselves on the brilliant getaway we had pulled off. We got bold. Too bold, it turns out.

On that day we walked into the mine along the tracks and worked our way closer and closer to the plant area. If you have seen a mining operation you may be familiar with their stockpiles. At the Empire they had a huge stockpile of pellets. Long conveyor systems high in the air reached out of the plant and spilled pellets into huge hills. I suppose they had to be fifty feet high or so. The point where the conveyor discharged the pellets was changed when the pile got to a certain height, so what you had was this long narrow hill of pellets with conical peaks all connected at the base. We just needed to get a real close look at this. When we got to it, we started to walk up the side. It was like trying to climb a pile of marbles. The pellets are not perfectly round, and they are rough, so they didn't roll away quite so easily as marbles would. But it was still sort of tricky to climb up the side of that hill. We got to laughing and pushing, and seeing who could climb higher, and by golly we got pretty high.

The mines have a PA system with microphones all over the place. If you needed someone you just walked up to one of these, pushed the button, and spoke into the mike. You said their name and your voice would be broadcast all over the mine. The person you paged would find another mike and talk back to you. I learned this later, of course, when I worked there.

As we romped on that pile of pellets we suddenly heard a voice boom out over that PA system. "THERE'S SOME G____ D____KIDS ON THE STOCK PILE."

It sounded much like our old friend from the X3R phone conversation. At least the tone and word selection was similar.

The three of us took immediate flight. If climbing a pile of marbles is tough, descending is a breeze, and we reached maximum flight speed very quickly. We hit the ground running, and as we did we saw a van leave the plant and begin winding its way towards us. We were headed to the fence, and it was a good distance away.

It seems we had to cross several sets of railroad tracks, all of which were on raised grades. The van was drawing closer. I don't remember if we made a plan together as we ran or just all reached the same strategy out of coincidence. Obviously when we went over the tops of those grades we were in plain sight, and just as obviously when we got down between them we were as good as invisible. The last obstacle to climb was the fence and this would not be so easy as running over a railroad track. We would be pretty conspicuous too, especially if we got hooked on the barbed wire strands at the top of the fence. So when we got between the last grade and the fence we just stopped and hid.

We ducked into some tall grass and laid low for some period of time. Things seemed quiet so I got up and moved slowly up the railroad grade to peer over the top to check on our pursuer. I neared the top of the slope and raised myself up and looked right into the face of a uniformed guy about ten feet away from me on the other side of the tracks. His van was parked several yards behind him, and it was a very official looking vehicle with company logos and such on it, and his uniform was very coplike. I don't remember a gun but there was a badge. The adrenaline began to surge through my system, my mind racing. If we bolted in different directions, two of us were likely to escape. After the BB gun thing I had no illusions about who wouldn't. After a few moments of high tension, I just surrendered. I didn't say anything nor do anything but I just sort of deflated, and the guy knew what I was doing. I started to recall my experience at the Negaunee Police Station. At least I hadn't shot at anybody this time.

My companions were right behind me, and it seems as though they went through much the same thought process as I did. We were caught. Mr. Mine Cop looked at us and said,

"You kids shouldn't be in here." Or something to that effect.

"Ok, we'll leave", we replied. The words may not be exact but you get the idea.

We made our way to the fence and climbed over. The Mine Cop watched us for a little while, and then drove off in his van. It was both amazing and disappointing. We didn't get arrested. We didn't get yelled at. What was up with that? The guy should have fired a gun into the air or something. At least he could have chewed us out.

I don't remember sneaking into the Empire after that. If we did I don't recall it. That would make sense because the possibility of capture by the mine cops had once made each trip an adventure. With that element of danger removed, I suppose sneaking into the mine became like a walk in the park or something. Walks in the park don't stay in your memory very long.

17

Goodbye to Bellevue

The land where all the homes in Bellevue stood was leased from the mining company that ran the Empire Mine. We owned our homes but not the land they were built on. From the time the Empire started up there was talk in the neighborhood that soon we would all be leaving. The way this worked for folks living on leased land was that the company would buy the home from the owner. From what I understand, they were given fair prices. Then the company would sell the home back to the owner for a dollar with the understanding that the owner would leave and remove the structure. It seems to me that everyone was actually excited about the possibility of moving. I know I was. I was now in junior high, and school activities and friends were becoming more prominent in my thinking. Moving to town appealed to me. Today I sort of scratch my head about that line of thinking.

There were already two empty houses in the valley. The old woman that had owned the little farm was long gone, and her home had been empty since she died. Another neighbor had moved away after her husband passed away. That was the situation when we heard the first news about someone receiving a buyout offer. It caused excitement in our homes.

If I recall correctly, it was my friend Kenny's family that got bought out and left first, moving to Palmer. I remember him telling me after the move how much there was to do in Palmer. Soon afterwards all the homeowners got their offers and began making their plans to leave. One of my best friends in school told me that the house next door to him was for sale. I told Mom and Dad and they looked at it and bought it. We were the first to leave the valley. In short order the families of Bellevue began scattering to go their separate ways. Nobody went very far. I don't recall where they all ended up, but except for Bill and Jennie's family, they all stayed in the Negaunee School District. The kids all continued on in Negaunee schools, and we kept in touch with them there. Bill and Jennie built a new home in Black River on the land where they had their camp.

Seven of the fourteen Prusi kids from Bellevue were already off on their own, and another was about to leave for college. That left six people in our household, and only four in Bill and Jennie's. Our new home in Negaunee had four bedrooms for the six of us so it was high living now with both Susie and I getting large bedrooms of our own.

The most difficult part of the move for me was that my folks didn't want to bring our dogs to town, and we had three of them. Two were young dogs and recent additions to our family so parting with them was not overly traumatic, especially when one went to a cousin and another to a school chum. But leaving my pal Tramp, who had been with us longer than any dog we had ever owned and with whom I had shared so many adventures, was terribly painful for me. I shed some pretty heartfelt tears the day we pulled out of Bellevue and left him temporarily with Bill and Jennie. Later some friends of my folks took him in. They had grandchildren, and I heard later that he was happy there.

While I looked forward to our move, the significance of leaving my childhood home was not completely lost on me. Not long before we moved I said a goodbye in my own way. Among my worldly treasures was a plastic sort of tablecloth. It was one of the many cereal box toys I acquired over the years. I mailed in my money for it after seeing it advertised on that cereal box. It was bright yellow, and on one side of it there was a checkerboard and other game tables printed in red. It was a multipurpose toy. I had not played with it much for a long time, so I decided to use it to leave a signature of sorts on Bellevue. I folded it in half with the red printing now on the inside and not visible. Using some paint or markers I wrote my name and made some fancy symbols befitting a flag. I got a length of two by two lumber and laid the edge of my flag on this wood, then put another piece of wood on top to sandwich the plastic sheet between the two wooden pieces and fastened this all together. I then walked up to the pines.

As you walked from our house up the road towards the highway, just opposite the old farmhouse, a small footpath led off to the right. This was the path to "the pines", and it was also a shortcut if you were walking towards Negaunee. I followed the well-worn path 'til I got to the pines. It was a small group of large pine trees. I think they were white pine but I can't remember for sure. The pines stood in a rough circle, and in the center of the circle there was no underbrush. The ground was covered with fallen leaves and a lot of pine needles. There were several large rocks in and around the circle of trees, some rather table-like. It was cool and shady. It was here that Rod and Doug and I had stashed the coffee cans full of cigarette butts that we had picked up along the highway so that we could learn to smoke. We had chewed on alder leaves afterwards to remove the smoke smell, but when Auntie Jennie suspected we were smoking and sniffed Doug's breath she said, "Alder leaves. You've been smoking!"

On the lower side of the pines, the side towards the houses and the crick, was a swamp. It was cool and there were yellow cowslips in the spring and jack-in-the pulpit later in the summer.

The Professor had showed me jack-in-the-pulpit and told me how tasty the stalks were to chew on. When I tried it he laughed as I started to chew, and then my whole mouth got tingly and started to burn. Once again the Professor had pulled my leg.

So to the pines I went with my flag, a hammer, and nails. I climbed one of the trees all the way to the top, like I had so many times before. The very top of the tree was dead or dying and free of needles and limbs. Here I nailed my yellow flag with my name on it. I was ready to leave now. I had left my signature.

Dad had decided that we would tear down the house and sell the lumber. I was almost old enough to hunt deer now, and he bought me a deer rifle as pay in advance for helping him with the project. This worked out real well, for the first day we came to work on it, some people came over and offered Dad some money for the house as is, and they would tear it down. Dad liked that idea and so did I, so I got my deer rifle for one day of not so hard labor. We stopped back another day, and the men had a lot of the place already ripped down. I walked around the house and laughed when I saw how they hung up their tools. They just smashed a hole in the interior wall with the tool and left it hanging there. Uncle Bill sold his house to someone who had it moved to a new foundation not far from Negaunee. It still stands there today, the only surviving home from Bellevue. Not long after we left, everyone was gone and all the structures torn down.

I made a couple of hunting and fishing excursions to Bellevue in the next couple of years. Once when I was a senior in high school I was taking pictures for the yearbook of a group of our students and foreign students taking a tour of the area. We rode buses to the Empire Mine and took a tour, then got to ride in the caboose of an ore train from the Empire to another facility in Negaunee. As the train left the mine I sort of forgot my assignment, as I wanted to see Bellevue as we passed through it. As we came within sight of my old stomping grounds, I pointed it out to the kids in the group. I was pretty excited to be getting a look at the valley again, especially from the vantagepoint of a moving train.

The kids looked and nodded but it was obvious they weren't interested. Why would they be? So I wormed my way up into the cupola on top of the caboose. I found a chair there where I could look out the window. I got into that spot about the time the train got to Bellevue. It was a lovely sunny day, and as we clacked down the tracks I had a wonderful view of the valley and surrounding country. I sat there in the spot where a lot of brakemen had sat and waved back at a bunch of little kids lined up to watch his train pass through Bellevue. I had been one of those kids on many occasions. The thrill of living in town had long since worn off for me, and as I watched our little valley passing by outside the window, I got to missing the place and wishing we had never left. It was the first time I remember feeling that way about Bellevue.

Right after graduation, several of my buddies and I made a three or four day camping trip to the valley. We pitched a tent on the hill and had a wonderful time being kids. We fished and climbed the bluff and played cowboys and Indians. We were way too old for that, and I think we knew it but wanted to be kids for just a little while longer. We knew there was a possibility that we might be "playing guns" for real before too long, as Viet Nam was a very real deal at the time. It was a great camping trip.

In the mid-seventies, my wife and I were visiting in the UP as were my sister Kathy and her husband. We decided to take a walk to Bellevue. We drove in from the Negaunee end as far as we could. There was a pile of dirt across the old highway where a dozer had just scooped a big chunk out of the road and piled it across the pavement as a barrier. There was also a fence across the road but it was knocked down on one side, and it was obvious that foot and bicycle traffic was going around the barrier. This was just the way it was when we left Bellevue.

It was a nice sunny day and we walked four abreast down old M35. Grass had begun to creep in over the edges of the pavement and up through cracks. Young trees had sprouted along the shoulders. We came to the barrier at the Bellevue end, and it too was like we remembered. No barrier at all really. We walked the long sweeping curve where the hardwoods reached out over the road and to the railroad crossing. The railroad crossing where I peeked out the car window at my dog Jip after he was killed by the school bus and where we found the neat little reflectors from the old crossing sign. It was here that we had wiped out a lot on our bikes when we hit the round iron ore pellets that had fallen from the cars and where that X3R phone was. Just past the crossing was the grove of trees where the ragamuffin sniper's reign of terror began and ended, and it was just as we passed these trees that we saw the pickup truck coming down the highway towards us. Mine Cop!

We were there in the wide open and trespassing on posted land. That same old feeling in my gut was happening. It looked like only one guy in the truck. I might not be able to outrun my brother-in-law Tim but I was pretty sure I could outrun both the girls. But I was an adult now, so we just walked off the pavement to the shoulder as he pulled up. I walked over to the driver as he rolled down his window and stopped. It was Matt, my friend Kenny's dad and former neighbor in Bellevue. He recognized me right away, and we smiled and said hello. I told him we were just taking a walk in to look at the old home place, and he said that wouldn't be a problem. We chatted a bit and he continued on his rounds, and we continued our walk.

Many of the elm trees that lined the road into the valley had died. There was little or nothing to see where the houses had stood. Some concrete from our sauna foundation was visible, and the old basketball backboard was still hanging on the tree, the plywood beginning to delaminate. What had been the field beyond Bill and Jennie's garden was growing up to brush and saplings and there was the Yodskof space capsule lying on its side. It was sort of a sad trip.

My last visit to the valley was a couple of years after that. Another brother-in-law and I decided to try some trout fishing on the crick. We walked in from the Negaunee end, and when we got near the valley I had him walk down to the crick while I continued to the upper end of Bellevue. I would start fishing where the crick crossed the road. Right near where we almost lost Doug and the Yodskof capsule that day. I would fish downstream as he fished upstream till we met. I was not able to execute my plan exactly, for when I got near the old bridge I could see a mountain of red brown rock burying the old bridge site. The crick was a trickle coming out a culvert pipe at the foot of this mountain. I began to walk the crick downstream but there was too little water to fish so it was just a hike. I met Bob at the old bridge in the valley. There was a pool there, and he had caught a small trout or two. He had started to walk upstream but saw it was a pretty futile exercise as far as catching fish.

We took a walk around the neighborhood. Not much had changed since my last visit. I got a picture of the bluff, and Bob took one of me standing on the cement base of our old sauna chimney. It sort of looks like a statue of me, and I tell everyone that that's what it is. We climbed the hill, and I tried to find my initials and the pictures that I had carved into the face of "Slide Rock". I had done this with a railroad spike and hammer and had pounded on that spike till my hands hurt, carving the lines deep into the soft rock. The rock chips really flew and stung my face when they hit it. I can remember what the pulverized rock smelled like and even what it tasted like for some of those chips landed in my mouth. I was lucky I didn't lose an eye. I was able to make out some of the carvings, but had I not known where to look and what to look for they would have gone unnoticed.

We tried to fish downstream on the way out but there was so little water that I couldn't even recognize the old swimming hole that my sister had "bought" from one of the neighbor boys for a dime. This was my last trip to the valley.

Bill and Jennie's kids made a trip to Bellevue together some time after this. Cousin Chas was working at the Empire now and knew that the valley would soon be buried under tons of rock, so he organized an excursion. They made a day of it and took a lot of pictures. That was the last visit for most of them.

Today, nobody would recognize the valley. Perhaps the bluff still dominates the landscape, but there is nothing to indicate that this valley was once the happy home of a half dozen families. It overlooks acres and acres of reddish brown rock. It is part of the moonscape that marks the outside edge of the Empire Mine.

18

All Grown Up

It has been thirty-five years since the little community of Bellevue ceased to exist. The former residents are scattered far and wide now, many of them gone from this earth. For me, our departure from the little valley coincided with another of life's crossroads. I was just about to enter high school. My move from Bellevue to Negaunee coincided with my move from childhood to young adulthood. When I talk about childhood I am talking about Bellevue, and when I dream of days gone by it is almost always Bellevue and not Negaunee. The older kids, my sisters and cousins, spent all or nearly all of their "at home" years in Bellevue, and even the youngest of the Bellevue Prusi kids, my sister Kelly, spent seven years there. For all of us and I imagine for the other kids who grew up in the neighborhood, Bellevue is remembered as a sort of idyllic place. Perhaps the fact that it is now gone, or at least unrecognizable, contributes to that impression. I can still go to Negaunee and walk my old haunts and even see the house there, but none of us can do that with Bellevue. Within a few years of leaving Bellevue, both my Dad and Uncle Bill passed away. Dad died in May of 1971 and Bill in December of the same year. The two couples had been married within months of each other, and now the two brothers departed from this earth within months of each other. As is often the case when such things happen, the families got a little nostalgic and as is proper, began to think more about the real important things in life. Shortly after losing Dad and Bill, the two families had a Christmas party together for the first time since we had left the valley. Not many years after that we had a summertime reunion and this has become a regular thing. One of the reunions coincided with an Olympic year, and we began to call our gathering the Elympics. We hold it every three to five years. In the early days we had a lot of athletic events, usually pitting the two families against each other. We initiated the new "outlaws" who had married into the family and had awards ceremonies with plenty of gag gifts. Most of this continues at the Elympics but the athletic events have, for the most part, been turned over to the younger generation. We last held the event in 2001, and most of the fourteen cousins got their exercise chasing their grandkids. We are pleased that the next generation and even the "outlaws" all seem to make a point of attending this event. We had 105 people that year, and if everyone showed up it would be around 130 now, including my Mom, who is the last survivor of the two couples who started all of this.

Had my siblings and I grown up next door to these same cousins in Brooklyn, New York, I imagine we would probably still be as close as we are today. But our shared memories would be a lot different, and I really think the place we came from was very special and added more to our shared experience than most other places would. The relationship is about the people and not places, but to have a special place in our backgrounds contributes much to our fond memories.

It is very difficult not to slip into stereotypical "old timer" mode when you write a story like this, and I am gonna just let myself slip. The world has changed so much. Society is much better in some ways, much worse off in others. There is amazing technology that can bring the world to a PC screen in your home, and the same technology can give kids access to things that no kid should see. The world is infinitely more complex. A childhood today seems in some ways a lot shorter than the one I had because of what kids see and experience now. At the same time, it appears kids are not made to be responsible until they are a lot older. This seems like sort of a bad mix to me. I suppose the sociologist will figure all of this out one day and give us a recipe to follow. I wonder how many kids today would choose to lay on their belly on a rock, looking down into a pool or a stream to watch a "walking stick" or a pollywog, instead of wiggling a joystick at a computer screen filled with amazing graphics and special effects. I wonder what I would have done if I had had the choice. How would it have affected who I've become?

There is no way that every child can have an untroubled childhood. The world will never be able or willing to give that to every child. It's too bad. Because if all children could grow up in a place like I did and with the adult influence that I had, there would be fewer angry people and fewer problems in this world.

At our last Elympics reunion, my cousin, Audrey (Prusi) Wright, read aloud a little essay she had written about our life in Bellevue. I was acting as the MC, and when "Auda" finished reading, we had to pause the program for a while to let people dry their eyes and because the MC was too choked up to speak. I want to close this story with the closing of that essay, and with her permission, here it is.

In Bellevue the two Prusi families spent all the birthdays and holidays together, as well as all the other days in between, like snow days spent at home from school, sick days when everyone shared the chicken pox or measles, rainy days, sunny days and sometimes even boring days when we whined and sighed, "What is there to do?" With so many shared times, a bond was created that still holds the families together now over forty years later. Retelling stories of those days is a favorite pastime when we are together. For us it's always fun to recapture the heart pounding fun and excitement of childhood and remember what a warm and wonderful feeling it was to wake up to huge snowdrifts on Christmas morning . . . and a light on in the window of that house next door.

The End

Order Form

For an autographed copy of:
Country Boy – Adventures from an Untroubled Childhood
Please copy this page, add the necessary information, and mail to:

Tales from Cedar Valley
PO Box 482
Floodwood, MN 55736

Please enclose personal check or money order, payable to:
Tales from Cedar Valley.

Name: _____

Address: _____

City: _____ State: _____ Zip: _____

Telephone: (_____) _____

Prices subject to change without notice.

Autographed Hardcover: $29.00 ea Qty. _____ Sub total: _____

Autographed Softcover: $19.00 ea Qty. _____ Sub total: _____

Minnesota residents please add 6.5% sales tax: _____

Shipping: $4.00 for first book and $2.00 each additional book: _____

Total Enclosed: _____